Devotions for Growing Christians

Devotions for Growing Christians

David R. Reid

LOIZEAUX BROTHERS

Neptune, New Jersey

FIRST EDITION, APRIL 1986

A publication of LOIZEAUX BROTHERS, Inc.
A Nonprofit Organization Devoted to the Lord's Work and to the Spread of His Truth

Library of Congress Cataloging-in-Publication Data
Reid, David R., 1937-
   Devotions for growing Christians.

   1. Christian life—1960–   .   2. Bible—Meditations. I. Title.
BV4501.2.R426   1986   242   86-140
ISBN 0-87213-701-5

PRINTED IN THE UNITED STATES OF AMERICA

Contents

Foreword

The first time I came across David Reid's "Devotions for Growing Christians," I was impressed by their solid spiritual content. Here was rich food for the soul.

Sometimes food can be served in an unappetizing manner—but not David Reid's. He serves it with a sprig of parsley. And I like the fact that the servings are modest in size. I don't always have time for a huge meal, but I have no trouble with these lunches.

It is also simple food. The author doesn't choke us with ponderous theological language. Like Spurgeon, he puts the food down where the lambs can reach it, knowing that it won't hurt the sheep to stoop.

Finally, I find the devotions to be timely. They deal with subjects that we need today in our spiritual diet. They speak to us where we are.

So I say what the French and others say at the beginning of every meal, "Bon appetit."

WILLIAM MACDONALD

1

Bags with Holes

Haggai 1:6, NIV   You earn wages, only to put
them in a [bag] with holes in it.
Read all of Haggai.

A bag with holes is not exactly the best place
for saving your hard earned cash. That's like collecting
water in a sieve—not too successful. But whoever does
such a stupid thing as to dump money into a bag with
holes? You and I do! When our priorities are not in
line with the teaching of the book of Haggai, we definitely "put our money into a bag with holes."

In order to better appreciate the teaching of this
Old Testament prophetic book, let us first consider its
historical background. The events of the little book of
Haggai took place relatively late in Old Testament history—about fifteen hundred years after Abraham,
about one thousand years after Moses and about five
hundred years after David. Haggai is known as a post-
exilic prophet because he preached and prophesied
after the Jewish people had returned from their sev-

enty years of captivity in Babylon. This return to the homeland was permitted by the benevolent decree of Cyrus, the Persian king who overthrew the Babylonian empire in 539 B.C. Approximately fifty thousand Jews returned to Jerusalem at that time under the leadership of Zerubbabel (Haggai 1:1).

With genuine thanksgiving to the Lord who had brought them safely home, these zealous Jews began to rebuild their temple. The altar was reconstructed, the offerings and feasts were reestablished, and the foundation of the new temple was completed. You can read all about this joyful time of thanksgiving and praise in Ezra 3. Unfortunately however, this revival atmosphere was short-lived. Enemy threats from neighboring nations as well as fear and frustration among the Jews themselves resulted in great discouragement and construction of the house of the Lord came to a complete standstill (see Ezra 4). For fifteen long years no work was done on God's house. It was left as an open and exposed foundation in the ground. And until the prophet Haggai arrived on the scene, the people of God had an "I-couldn't-care-less" attitude toward the whole fiasco of rebuilding (Haggai 1:2).

How tragic and yet how familiar even today. How often we see the work of the Spirit of God quenched and stifled after the laying of a promising foundation. Many Christians have a good firm foundation in the faith but are no longer growing Christians. They started out with a lot of zeal and enthusiasm and praise but are not building any more. Their once solid foundation now lies exposed to the weathering effects of this world's system of values and attitudes. Is it possible that your spiritual building program has been discontinued and your foundation has been forgotten?

What about your prayer time and your time for reading God's Word each day? Is there continuous construction going on or is there a general strike?

The same kinds of questions could be asked of many of our churches and fellowship groups. Is building activity progressing or are we looking at abandoned foundations? Are we concerned about the continued need for teaching and worship, fellowship and prayer? (See Acts 2:42 for these necessary building materials.) We must all ask ourselves whether we are actively involved in a building program for our fellowship or whether we are content to sit on the sidelines and see an exposed and crumbling foundation. Is it possible that our situation is even worse than this? Are we somehow hindering the building that God is doing through our fellow believers?

Why had the building of the temple stopped? Why did the people have such an apathetic attitude toward God's house? The answer is found in Haggai's scathing sermon which is given in verses 3-11 of chapter 1. The problem was priorities. God's people were spending much more time and effort and money on their own houses than on the house of the Lord (verse 4). A paneled house in Haggai's day was a sign of luxury because the expensive cedar timber had to be imported all the way from Lebanon in the north. God saw this materialistic, luxurious living as inconsistent with His building code standards. The people were told in no uncertain terms to reexamine their priorities and to give careful thought to their ways (verses 5 and 7).

Certainly there are lessons in this ancient sermon for the twentieth century Christian. God's living Word never ages. Do we have "paneled housing" priorities? Are we putting our own building projects ahead of

God's building program? Our building projects can be more than just literal houses. We can spend all kinds of building time and energy on our businesses or books or bankrolls or even our bodies, while the Lord's building work is neglected and left unattended.

Remember that it was not wrong for the people of Haggai's day to have houses, and there was nothing intrinsically wrong with cedar paneling. The problem was priorities. There was absolutely no work being done on the house of God. The open foundation of the temple was staring God's people in the face, yet they continued unashamedly to expend their time, energy, and money on their own houses. Priorities continue to be the number one problem for many of God's people today. Most Christians are not involved in glaring sins like adultery or blasphemy. And there is nothing inherently evil about spending time on our businesses, books, bankrolls, and bodies! But it is a sin to put any of these things higher on the priority list than our worship and service to God. Do we? We may say that this would never happen in our lives. However, a brief examination of our priority list based on time allotment or energy consumption may surprise us. The Word of the Lord is: "Give careful thought to your ways."

The full tragedy of the situation in the days of Haggai was not only that the house of God was forgotten but that the people of God were involved in a losing proposition. Because of their inverted priorities, the Lord had withheld His blessing on their land. Their herds were unproductive and their harvests were puny. The people were investing a great deal of time and labor to get ahead but there was no progress. In essence they were throwing their money into a bag with holes. Reversed priorities always lead to a bag with holes! When we replace the interests of God with our own interests, invariably we face disappointment and loss. Although there may be some short-term gains in pleasure or popularity or prosperity, ultimately wrong priorities result in no gain at all. How many of your future investments will end up in a bag with holes?

The Word of God never points out a problem without giving a solution. The solution to the problem of priorities is simply to reverse them. God's simple, straightforward solution for Haggai's day was systematically laid out before the people: "Go up into the mountains and bring down timber and build the house" (Haggai 1:8). The answer seems so obvious that we wonder why God had to say it. God said it because His people then were like His people now—slow to learn! Sometimes we are so thickheaded that God has to teach us the ABC's of Christian living again and again before we straighten out our priorities. When will we ever learn that we cannot expect smooth sailing all the time in the Christian life? The New Testament is filled with verses that teach us that our faith will be tested for our own good by trials and persecutions. (See John 15:20; John 16:33; Acts 14:22; 1 Thessalonians 3:3; 2 Timothy 3:12; James 1:2; 1 Peter 1:6-7; 1 Peter 2:21; 1 John 3:13.)

The wonderful response of the people to Haggai's ministry is given to us in the remainder of this little book of Scripture. A response to preaching is not always so positive, but this case should be an encouragement to servants of the Lord today who are somewhat discouraged and maybe even doubting the possibility of God's working through preaching. As a result of Haggai's sermon, the people showed reverence for the Lord, they were stirred up in spirit, and they returned to the work of the house of the Lord (Haggai 1:12-15). What a remarkable change of attitude—from irreverent apathy to reverent action. It's not impossible today!

In chapter 2 we read of the continuing ministry of Haggai while the temple was being completed. The people were encouraged with promises about the future and challenged to continue holy living. We learn from Ezra 6:15 that the temple was not completed overnight but took about four years to finish. Those four years were years of blessing on the land and on the people (Haggai 2:19), because they were years of right priorities. No longer were the investments of God's people going into a bag with holes. May the people of God today also take seriously the words of the prophet Haggai. Then, as a result, we will hear the voice of the Lord saying: "From this day on I will bless you" (verse 19).

2

Short Christians

Ephesians 6:21-22   But that you may also
know about my circumstances, how I am
doing, Tychicus, the beloved brother and
faithful minister in the Lord, will make
everything known to you. And I have sent
him to you for this very purpose, so that you
may know about us, and that he may comfort
your hearts.

Philippians 2:25-30   But I thought it
necessary to send to you Epaphroditus, my
brother and fellow-worker and fellow-soldier,
who is also your messenger and minister to
my need; because he was longing for you all
and was distressed because you had heard that
he was sick. For indeed he was sick to the
point of death, but God had mercy on him,
and not on him only but also on me, lest I
should have sorrow upon sorrow. Therefore I
have sent him all the more eagerly in order
that when you see him again you may rejoice
and I may be less concerned about you.
Therefore receive him in the Lord with all
joy, and hold men like him in high regard;
because he came close to death for the work
of Christ, risking his life to [make up for the
help you could not give me].

Colossians 4:12-13   Epaphras, who is one

of your number, a bondslave of Jesus Christ,
sends you his greetings, always laboring
earnestly for you in his prayers, that you may
stand perfect and fully assured in all the will
of God. For I bear him witness that he has a
deep concern for you and for those who are
in Laodicea and Hierapolis.

Have you heard that song "Short People"? It's
quite a satirical criticism of people who are physically
small. Many short people laugh along with the rest of
the listeners and even like the song, but there are
some who become upset with the song because it
makes them feel inferior and degraded.

Some Christians have a "short-people" complex—
not because of physical measurements but because of
spiritual qualifications. These Christians feel inferior
and put down because they visualize themselves as below normal in natural talent or spiritual gift. Of course
the Bible assures us that there is no such thing as an
inferior or insignificant or unimportant Christian. Every Christian has a responsibility in the kingdom of
God and a function in the body of Christ. However,
there is always the tendency for the growing Christian
who is not loaded with unusual natural talent or out-
going personality or an obvious spiritual gift to feel
"short." Do you ever feel that way—inferior, insignificant, unimportant? Does the question, "Where was I
when the Lord passed out the gifts and talents?" ever
cross your mind? Well, take heart, because the Bible
indicates that "short" Christians are very important

and very necessary for the proper functioning of any Christian ministry.

In the Scriptures mentioned above we have three "short" Christians who were associated with the apostle Paul: Tychicus, Epaphroditus, and Epaphras. Paul was the dynamic leader and the center of attention; Paul was the great teacher and preacher and missionary; Paul was the outstanding gift which the risen and ascended Christ gave to His church. But there were many "little people" connected with the great apostle. Their names appear very briefly on the pages of Scripture, but enough is said about them to show us that they were a very important and necessary part of the ministry. Tychicus, Epaphroditus, and Epaphras are just three of these "short" Christians who were used by the Lord for special and significant service.

Tychicus was a "beloved brother" (Ephesians 6:21). He was the kind of Christian you like to have around— good attitude, helpful, easy to love. Not all Christians bring with them an atmosphere of love. We need more beloved brothers and sisters like Tychicus. They are the all-important and necessary "oil" in the "machinery" of Christian ministry. Are you a "beloved brother" or are other Christians glad to see you move on?

We also read that Tychicus was a "faithful servant." He was dependable and reliable. He could be trusted to get the job done. No wonder Paul chose him to carry both the Ephesian and the Colossian letters (Colossians 4:7-8). Suppose this mail had been lost! Little did Tychicus realize how important a role he was playing in God's plan for completing the Scriptures. Perhaps the insignificant things the Lord has called you to are far more significant and important than you ever imagined. In 2 Timothy 4:12 we learn that Tychicus was faithful right to the end. 2 Timothy was written by the apostle Paul from a dungeon in Rome just a few months before he was martyred. By this time many believers had forsaken Paul for one reason or another (see 2 Timothy 1:15 and 4:10), but Tychicus remained faithful. Dependability and reliability are needed more than ever in the Christian ministry today. The "grass is always greener" or the ministry more exciting someplace other than the little neighborhood fellowship or local church Bible study where you are now. But this may be exactly the ministry where the Lord expects you to be faithful week by week.

One other thing we learn about Tychicus from Ephesians 6:22 is that he was able to bring comfort or encouragement to fellow believers. He was not only a letter and information carrier; he was a comforter. Brother Tychicus had just the right personality and demeanor and concise words necessary to encourage other Christians. Maybe you're like Tychicus. Many Christians whose gifts and talents are more publicly visible are misfits when it comes to comforting fellow believers in times of sorrow or stress. Perhaps the Lord has gifted you with the unique ability to comfort that Christian friend whose father has just died or to encourage that believer who is wavering in the faith. What an important and significant ministry!

In Philippians 2:25-30 we read of another "short" Christian who was associated with the apostle Paul. His name was Epaphroditus. The church at Philippi had sent him to deliver a financial gift for Paul's ministry. No sooner had Epaphroditus arrived in Rome than he became very sick and almost died (verse 27). Epaphroditus was upset about this because he thought that the home church would look on him as a failure. They had entrusted him with a simple mission and he couldn't even stay healthy long enough to make the round trip! Epaphroditus was quite dejected and demoralized at this point (verse 26). What good was he for anything, let alone Christian service? Have you ever felt like Epaphroditus? Everyone else seems to be able to do a normal job for Christ but you always fail in one way or another—you even get sick at the wrong times!

But wait a minute! Before you give up entirely, take a look at the divine commentary on Epaphroditus in verses 29-30. This "short" Christian was to be held in high regard. He was to be given a hero's welcome when he returned home. Why? Because he risked his life for the work of Christ. Epaphroditus wasn't knifed on a street corner in Rome for preaching the gospel, and he wasn't thrown into the arena with savage lions for the sake of his faith. No—he just got very sick in his job of Christian service. Maybe he caught the Roman flu! God's view of Epaphroditus should be a real encouragement to us. Epaphroditus thought of himself as a failure, but God's Word honors him as having traveled the road of a martyr for Jesus Christ. What a blessing for growing Christians to realize! Of course we should take reasonable care of the bodies that the Lord has given us, but if we face danger or illness in the course of serving the Lord we can be sure that God counts it as suffering for His sake. Experiencing burn-out for Christ is commendable!

Epaphras was still another "short" Christian who worked with the great apostle Paul. Epaphras was not a great teacher or a great preacher but rather a great prayer. Colossians 4:12-13 tells us that he labored earnestly in prayer for his fellow believers. How often do we labor in prayer for fellow Christians? We must confess that too often our prayers are self-centered—our problems, our needs, our wants. When was the last time we reached out in our own private prayers to pray for the spiritual growth of brothers and sisters that we know? Have we ever "labored earnestly" in our prayers for other believers—maybe even to the point of tears? Laboring in prayer for others is a very important part of the Christian ministry, and it is one that we can all perform regardless of our natural talents or spiritual gifts.

Epaphras is also mentioned in Philemon verse 23. Here Paul refers to him as "my fellow prisoner." Now this is quite interesting. When Paul wrote Philemon (as well as Ephesians, Philippians, and Colossians, which are known as the four prison Epistles) he was under house arrest in Rome. This meant that he was free to live in his own rented quarters but he was chained to a Roman guard at all times. Under these trying conditions Paul wrote and spread the gospel while he waited for his trial before Caesar (Acts 28:30-31). The fact that Paul refers to Epaphras as "my fellow prisoner" indicates that most likely Epaphras voluntarily submitted himself to imprisonment in order to assist the apostle in that situation. Perhaps he and Aristarchus (another "short" Christian referred to as "my fellow prisoner" in Colossians 4:10) took different shifts and, among other things, wrote for Paul as his secretaries. In any case it appears that Epaphras voluntarily gave up his own freedom to assist Paul. Would you do that: give up your freedom to help another Christian in his ministry? Or would you feel that you would rather be selfish and make a name for yourself in Christian circles? Perhaps God is calling you to a supporting role in some Christian ministry—behind the scenes, but very important.

No Christian should have a "short people" complex. God's Word shows us that "short" Christians are not inferior or insignificant or unimportant. In fact, all Christians are potential "giants" in Christian faith and ministry as far as God is concerned!

3

Treasure in Jars of Clay

2 Corinthians 4:7-12, NIV   But we have this treasure in jars of clay to show that this all-surpassing power is from God and not from us. We are hard pressed on every side, but not crushed; perplexed, but not in despair; persecuted, but not abandoned; struck down, but not destroyed. We always carry around in our body the death of Jesus, so that the life of Jesus may also be revealed in our body. For we who are alive are always being given over to death for Jesus' sake, so that His life may be revealed in our mortal body. So then, death is at work in us, but life is at work in you.

There will be changes in our lives this year! This is not a trite prophecy taken from a Chinese fortune cookie, but rather it is a fact of life. Nothing in this life stays the same. We will all change in certain ways during this year. The big question is—will we *grow* as Christians?

2 Corinthians 4:7-12 has a few important things to say to us about Christian growth. What is said is both encouraging and disturbing. How encouraging it is to know that the power for growth in the Christian life is not self-generated, but comes from God Himself (verse 7). And this power is really there within every Christian, even though it is placed in such unlikely common containers as you and I! But this Scripture is also disturbing because it is a blow to our pride to admit that we are nothing but jars of clay! And not only that, but it seems that God purposely permits these frail jars to be battered (verses 8-9) and broken (verses 10-11). Is this Christian *growth,* you ask? Yes! Let's look at this passage in more detail.

The theme of this section of Scripture is the extreme contrast between the message of the gospel (see verse 6) and the messenger of the gospel. The fantastic and fabulous message of the good news in Jesus Christ is carried by frail and fragile messengers. The main point is that God has purposely designed it this way so that there will be no mistake as to the source of the great life-changing power of the gospel of the Lord Jesus Christ. This point is illustrated in verse 7 by the contrast between a treasure and a clay jar.

At the time that this Scripture was written, earthenware vessels were very plentiful in that part of the world. They were used as containers to hold water or food. Sometimes these clay pots were used to hold things of greater worth, such as money, jewels, or even parchments. (The Dead Sea Scrolls were found in such containers.) The common lamp at that time was also an earthenware vessel. It was composed of a cheap clay pitcher or jar containing olive oil and a floating wick. All of these pottery vessels were easy to purchase and broke just as easily. In fact, such potsherds can still be seen among ancient ruins today.

Thus the contrast between the carrier and the content of the Christian message is well-illustrated. The message of the gospel is precious and valuable like a treasure of jewels or light, but it is purposely contained in common and ordinary looking human "vessels of clay." And "clay jars" are not supermen! They get runny noses and rashes. They are subject to flu and forgetfulness. Some people have the idea that the growing Christian is to become more like a "six million dollar man" each day. Not so! Although the power of the gospel is supernatural, the preacher (that's you and me!) is purposely not a superman.

In verses 8 and 9 the apostle Paul, the author of 2 Corinthians, proceeds to show that the Christian is not only a common earthenware container but is a battered container as well. He mentions instances in his own life which were impossible situations for mere man. The deliverances which he experienced were clearly brought about by the power of God and not by the genius of man. In these two verses, four sets of words are used to describe the battering of the clay vessel on the one hand and the miraculous deliverance by the power of God on the other hand.

"Hard pressed," "perplexed," "persecuted," and "struck down" all refer to the battering which a Christian undergoes as a messenger of the gospel. Can you identify with any of these words? What about the time you felt so depressed and discouraged that you didn't know which way to turn ("hard pressed, perplexed")? What about the time you tried to share your faith with that person who mocked you ("persecuted, struck down")?

"But not crushed," "but not in despair," "but not abandoned," and "but not destroyed" all refer to the deliverance which God is able to bring to any "impossible" situation. We can all think of times when God stepped into our situation and "saved the day." Remember the time when God "coincidentally" brought just the verse of Scripture you needed to your attention? Has there been a traumatic situation in your life through which you sensed the presence of Christ with you in a new way? Has there ever been a situation in which all natural means were at an end and, to your amazement, you saw the power of God at work in an unbelieveable way? God intentionally permits the clay pots to be battered so that He can exhibit His supernatural power in the situation.

In verses 10 and 11 God's purpose is further emphasized. The battering a Christian goes through has the result of breaking open the clay jar so that the treasure within can be seen. Even though the anxiety of circumstances, the antagonism of persons, and the attacks of Satan himself are deathblows to the natural human vessel of clay, the very life of Jesus is revealed through the Christian as a result. To "carry around in our body the dying of Jesus" and to be "given over to death for Jesus' sake" is to experience in some small way the battering which our Lord went through when He walked on this earth. The Christian who is seeking to live a godly life will in some way know what the hate of the world and the attack of Satan are all about. (See John 15:18 and 1 Peter 5:8.)

As the Christian undergoes these deadly attacks and the jar of clay is broken down, the divine life (which can never be destroyed) can be both seen and communicated more easily to others who need this treasure. In verse 12 Paul says that the breaking process at work in his life resulted in new life in Christ for the Corinthians (John 12:24). Will new life come to someone because Jesus has been seen in your life—through a broken jar of clay?

Throughout this year God will permit the battering and breaking process to go on in your life. There may be changes in your way of living, but that is all part of Christian growth. Remember, there is *treasure* that can meet the needs of others in your jar of clay.

4

The Cost of Disobedience

Jonah 1:1-5   The word of the LORD came
to Jonah the son of Amittai saying, "Arise, go
to Nineveh the great city, and cry against it,
for their wickedness has come up before Me."
But Jonah rose up to flee to Tarshish from
the presence of the LORD. So he went down to
Joppa, found a ship which was going to
Tarshish, paid the fare, and went down into it
to go with them to Tarshish from the
presence of the LORD. And the LORD hurled a
great wind on the sea and there was a great
storm on the sea so that the ship was about
to break up. Then the sailors became afraid,
and every man cried to his god, and they
threw the cargo which was in the ship into
the sea to lighten it for them. But Jonah had
gone below into the hold of the ship, lain
down, and fallen sound asleep.

The story of Jonah has probably been ridiculed
more than any other account in the Old Testament.
How could a man possibly be swallowed by a fish and

live? Even some Christians have a hard time "swallowing" this story and have called it merely an Old Testament parable. No! The book of Jonah is the historical account of a real man who lived in the eighth century B.C. (See 2 Kings 14:25.) Our Lord Jesus had no doubts about Jonah and his traumatic experience. In fact, He used it to predict and illustrate His own coming death and resurrection (Matthew 12:38-41).

There are many lessons we can learn from the life of Jonah. God has included the story of this prophet of Israel in the Bible so that growing Christians in the twentieth century may learn what God expects of His servants. Jonah was a servant of God, but he disobeyed the Word of the Lord and fled toward Tarshish instead of preaching at Nineveh. In His mercy, God reached down and brought Jonah back where he belonged, but it took a very thorough shake-up in the life of the prophet. (Read the entire book of Jonah.) The experiences Jonah went through were all part of the cost of disobedience. As servants of our Lord Jesus Christ, we are to be obedient to His Word. When we disobey, there is a cost involved. Yes, God will always reach down in love and completely forgive us and bring us back, but there are always consequences to forgiven sin.

Part of the cost of disobedience is separation. When, in disobedience, Jonah "rose up to flee," it was "from the presence of the Lord" (Jonah 1:3). Of course Jonah could not literally escape from God, but there was a separation as far as fellowship with God was concerned. Disobedience results in broken fellowship with the Lord.

Is it because of disobedience in your life that the

Lord seems so far away at times? What about the matter of family relationships? (See Ephesians 5:22-6:4.) What about forgiving one another? (See Colossians 3:12-13.) What about the question of friendship with the world? (See James 4:4.) Jesus said, "He who has My commandments, and keeps them, he it is who loves Me; and he who loves Me shall be loved by My Father, and I will love him, and will disclose Myself to him" (John 14:21). Obedience is the secret to intimate fellowship with our Lord.

The cost of disobedience also includes the danger of shipwreck. The ship in which Jonah was traveling "was about to break up" (Jonah 1:4). The disobedient Christian runs the risk of throwing his whole life of Christian service down the drain. Note that it is the Lord who hurls out the great wind which brings the storm. God did not purposely want to shipwreck Jonah. This was discipline! God was acting to bring Jonah back. If we disobey the Lord, He may permit our lives to be disrupted so that we will turn back to Him. Hebrews 12:6 says that "those whom the Lord loves He disciplines." There may be quite a "great storm" before the power struggle is over. But if we persist in our disobedience and refuse to humble ourselves, our life of service for Him may end in shipwreck.

More of the cost of disobedience is seen in verse 5. Other lives were also endangered because of Jonah's disobedience. We may ask ourselves: How many other lives are messed up because of *my* disobedience? Is my roommate still not a Christian because my life of disobedience is inconsistent with what I preach? Are there shattered relationships in my family because I refuse to submit to God's commandments for family life? Is there someone who has been badly hurt because I have been disobedient in my sex life? What a network of tragedies we build when we are disobedient Christians.

Finally, the cost of disobedience involves sleep. Verse 5 states that "Jonah had gone below into the hold of the ship, lain down, and fallen sound asleep." What a picture of the disobedient Christian! He is hardened and asleep to the claims and commands of the Lord. Meanwhile, the sailors are struggling for their lives. Jonah has the answer, but he's fast asleep! Like Jonah, we have the answer to man's struggle, but like Jonah, we often are unconcerned. People all around us are "afraid and crying out to their gods," desperately trying to maintain meaning and purpose and direction in this life. On the surface, many of them seem to be "expert sailors," but they really don't have the right answers. We have the only answer, but we sleep on! What a serious and sorrowful situation it is when we hold back the answer because of indifference. This hardened condition of our hearts is the result of disobeying our Lord. Loss of sensitivity is part of the cost of disobedience.

The cost of disobedience is high. Many times it is not easy to follow and obey the Word of the Lord, but how much better it is to suffer for the sake of obedience than to suffer the consequences of disobedience. (See 1 Corinthians 11:31-32.) If you have disobeyed the Lord in some area of your life, repent and confess this sin now. Our heavenly Father will always forgive and restore us completely as He did with Jonah. Continuing in disobedience is a serious mistake in the life of the growing Christian. Jonah "paid the fare" of disobedience—and so will every disobedient Christian.

5

Problems on Purpose

James 1:2-8   Consider it all joy, my
brethren, when you encounter various trials:
knowing that the testing of your faith
produces endurance. And let endurance have
its perfect result, that you may be perfect and
complete, lacking in nothing. But if any of
you lacks wisdom, let him ask of God, who
gives to all men generously and without
reproach, and it will be given to him. But let
him ask in faith, without any doubting, for
the one who doubts is like the surf of the sea
driven and tossed by the wind. For let not
that man expect that he will receive anything
from the Lord, being a double-minded man,
unstable in all his ways.

Problems and disappointments come in all
sizes! There are the large ones like the tragic death of
a friend or the unhappy breakup of a love relationship.
Then there are the medium-sized ones like the can-
cellation of a spring vacation trip. And there are the

small ones too, like standing in line or losing your keys or just having the rainy day blues.

Does the Bible have anything to say about these trials and tribulations? Yes it does, and the first chapter of James is one of these places. Let's see what this Scripture has to say about problems.

The first thing we learn from this passage is that a Christian should expect such problems. Verse 2 says "*when* you encounter various trials," not "*if* you encounter various trials." The disappointments of life confront the Christian the same as they do anyone else.

However, there is a difference between a believer's problems and disappointments and a nonbeliever's frustrations and anxieties. A Christian can meet the trials of life with joy—of all things! We are told in verse 2 that we can "consider it all joy" when our world appears to be caving in around us. Now God does not mean that we should jump up and down and shout "Praise the Lord!" when we find ourselves in the hospital because of a car accident or when our career plans fall through because a job application was rejected. No, but we can "consider it all joy" because we *know* (verse 3) that God has a purpose in every problem He permits to come our way. Nothing happens by chance or takes God by surprise. He is always in control of our situation. However, through the interaction of many different factors, He does allow certain problems to enter our lives—*problems on purpose!*

A number of God's purposes in the trials and tribulations of life are given in the Bible. Verses 3 and 4 of our Scripture give two of these purposes. First, there is the purpose of the "testing of your faith." God tests and proves our faith! How pure and genuine is my faith? Will it disappear under the pressure of circumstances? Would the sudden and shocking news that I had terminal cancer leave me quiet and submissive under the sovereign hand of God or shaking my fist in bitter rebellion at my Creator? 1 Peter 1:7 tells us that the testing of our faith is more precious than gold even though it is tested by fire. The thought here is that God applies the "heat" to refine our faith just as a precious metal is refined in a crucible. As the heat is applied, the impurities are burned off but the pure metal remains. Only now can the face of the refiner be reflected from the surface of the molten metal. Is the reflection of the Refiner seen in your life? (See also Psalm 66:10 and 2 Corinthians 4:11.)

A further purpose for the problems and disappointments of life is given in James 1:3-4. Our faith is not only tested and refined—it is made stronger. This is the thought in the phrases "produces endurance" and "that you may be perfect and complete, lacking in nothing." God does not want "jellyfish" children in His family. He wants us to be strong and mature, stable and balanced and well-rounded sons and daughters. Without the problems of life we would not develop endurance. Sickness and suffering and sorrow have a way of strengthening our faith in the Lord. The dark clouds bring the rains which are necessary for growing stronger. God uses the "April showers bring May flowers" principle in the spiritual lives of His children as well as in the physical life of His creation.

"And *let* endurance have its perfect result . . ." means don't rebel against God's way of working in your life. As mentioned above, a traumatic experience can leave you an angry and bitter critic of God or it can leave you a stronger and more mature believer in Him.

It all depends on whether you yield and submit and "let" His purpose have its "perfect result" or not.

Verse 5 is both a promise and a comfort. In the context of this part of God's Word, it means that if you need wisdom as to why God has allowed certain problems in your life you may ask Him and He will answer. Do you need understanding of a particular tragedy or disappointment in your life? Don't let it bother you! If you ask in faith (verse 6) the Lord will let you in on the inside track of what's going on. He may not give us *specific* reasons for what's happening (most likely they are too complicated for us to understand—see Isaiah 55:9), but He will give us spiritual insight and wisdom as to what's happening. And our heavenly Father never puts us down for coming and asking for this wisdom. He gives "generously and without reproach." What a comforting promise!

But too often we're like the man described in verses 6-8. We don't wait patiently by faith for the Lord's answer. We waver and we squirm and we complain and we cry and we demand like spoiled brats instead of maturing sons and daughters. No wonder verse 7 tells us that we shouldn't expect to receive the Lord's wisdom if we act like that!

The problems and disappointments in a Christian's life don't just happen at random. Although the following saying may be trite, it is right on the mark. "Our disappointments are His appointments." It's another way of saying "problems on purpose."

6
The Five W's

Habakkuk 2:4b, KJV   The just shall live by
[his] faith.
Read Habakkuk 2:1-4.

Habakkuk sounds like a name for chronic ar-
thritis, but it really is a book in the Bible! Look it up
in your table of contents and then read the whole
book—it's only three chapters—and you'll gain a
much greater appreciation of what's going on in the
few verses mentioned above.

Habakkuk was a prophet to Judah (southern Israel
with its capital at Jerusalem) during the seventh century B.C. Things were really bad in his day. There was
oppression of the poor and other social injustices. The
laws were either ignored or were twisted and manipulated in favor of the "filthy few." There was violence
in the streets. Corruption abounded. There was unrest
of every sort. Moral values had disintegrated. Only a
small minority was still holding on to faith in God. A
breakdown of society was taking place before Habak-

kuk's very eyes (verses 1-4). No wonder the sensitive heart of faithful Habakkuk cried out: "How long, O LORD, will I call for help?" (verse 2). How could God allow such open sin to go unjudged?

Certainly the Christian today can identify with Habakkuk. What better description can we get of the contemporary conditions in our communities or in our country than seen in Habakkuk 1:1-4? The soul of the sensitive Christian questions along with Habakkuk: "Why dost Thou make me see iniquity and cause me to look on wickedness?" (verse 3).

God answered Habakkuk's question, but the answer was a real shock for the prophet. "You haven't seen anything yet!" is essentially the Lord's answer in verses 5-11. Habakkuk was told that the wicked and violent and dreaded Chaldeans (the rising Babylonian empire) would overrun Judah. God would actually raise up a pagan nation to judge the sin which was rampant in the land. Again the parallel is too close to avoid mentioning. Is God permitting the rise of godless communism for the express purpose of judging a country which is rapidly departing from the faith that once characterized it? Habakkuk received the message, but didn't quite comprehend it. He realized that God had chosen this method of discipline when he responded: "Thou, O LORD, hast appointed them (Chaldeans) to judge; and Thou, O Rock, hast established them to correct" (verse 12). But what Habakkuk couldn't understand was how God could do such a thing! "Why dost Thou look with favor on those who deal treacherously? Why art Thou silent when the wicked swallowed up those more righteous than they?" (verse 13). How can a holy God permit an even more wicked nation than Judah to flourish and take over? Yes, Judah deserves her punishment, but why not the Chaldeans? They're much worse than we are. Doesn't this sound familiar?

Habakkuk was not the first to *wrestle* with questions of this sort. A man named Asaph had really struggled with this before. (See Psalm 73.) Nor was Habakkuk the last believer to wrestle with the whole question of evil. Every growing Christian must grapple at some point with this issue.

The position that Habakkuk took as he reflected upon his unanswered question is beautiful. That's what chapter 2:1-4 is all about. Habakkuk decided that he would simply wait patiently and watch intently for the Lord's answer. He didn't become frustrated and demand answers of God. He didn't give up with a "God doesn't care about my problems" attitude. No, he *waited* and *watched.* If only we could do the same with all our "why's?" and "how come's?"

The guard post or watchtower (note: not an ivory tower) was a place from which the watcher could see all around and better discern what was happening as well as guard his own position. This pictures for us the attitude that God would like us to take as we wait for answers to situations we can't understand. Don't stay down on the plain where you can't see very far! Come up to the tower where it's a little easier to catch God's view of what's happening. (It was only when Asaph went into the sanctuary that he perceived the answer from the Lord. See Psalm 73:16-17.) It is possible to turn unanswered questions over to the Lord and wait and watch for His answer. And while we're waiting, let's not give up an inch of ground of our faith in God just because we have some unanswered questions. The watchtower is also a guard post. Guard the truth that God has already given you.

God answered Habakkuk. God always answers the waiting and watching Christian. The answer was not: "Did He really answer me or was it only my pre-programmed imagination?" God doesn't send cryptograms for answers! The answer God gave Habakkuk was so clear that it could be written down and passed on to others. In fact, God wanted the answer to be broadcast without any waste of time (Habakkuk 2:2). Here is the answer that God gave to Habakkuk as to the perplexing problem of evil. Evil does exist (it is not imaginary), but it will exist for a limited time only—and that time is appointed by God. History is not haphazard but is moving toward a goal and there is no way that God's purpose can be threatened or thwarted. It will certainly come to pass right on His (not our) schedule (verse 3). When verse 3 here is quoted in Hebrews 10:37 the "it" becomes "He." The goal of history is centered in a person: the Lord Jesus Christ. All evil will be overcome, and Christ will be Lord of all.

What is the Christian to do in the meantime? He is to *walk* by faith (verse 4). We may not understand how a holy God can tolerate the existence of evil and why the wrong person always seems to get the best deal, but the righteous person (and what better deal is there than to be declared righteous by God?) shall live by his faith.

In the five woes that are pronounced upon the Chaldeans (verses 5-19) there is contained a universal principle. God assures us that everything evil is under the judgment of God. The seed of self-destruction is in the very soul of the person who is not right with God (verse 4). Final judgment is sure to come, but in the meantime the Christian is to be walking by his faith.

In chapter 3 of Habakkuk we see the prophet *worshiping* the Lord. This should be the outcome of all our wrestlings with God, but too often we become bitter and angry because we don't like to wait and watch and walk. Habakkuk's worship really began in verse 20: "The LORD is in His holy temple; let all the earth be silent before Him." Habakkuk learned to silently submit to God's divine rule and judgment—this is worship. He realized that his only approach to God was a plea for mercy (Habakkuk 3:2)—this is worship. He was awed by the glory of God (verses 3-4)—this is worship. He reflected on the great acts of God in history (verses 5-15)—this is worship. He trembled because he had gone through a deep spiritual experience and he had come to know the reality of a living God who was coming in judgment (verse 16)—this is worship. He rejoiced because he knew that in spite of the hard times and difficulties that are a result of evil, the Lord was still his strength and salvation (verses 17-19)–this is worship. "*Yet* I will exult in the Lord" (verse 18). This kind of worship comes only from the heart of one who has wrestled, waited, watched, and walked.

7

He Touched Me

Luke 5:12-14   And it came about that
while He was in one of the cities, behold,
there was a man full of leprosy; and when he
saw Jesus, he fell on his face and implored
Him, saying, "Lord, if You are willing, You
can make me clean." And He stretched out
His hand, and touched him, saying, "I am
willing; be cleansed." And immediately the
leprosy left him. And He ordered him to tell
no one, "But go and SHOW YOURSELF TO
THE PRIEST, and make an offering for your
cleansing, just as Moses commanded, for a
testimony to them.

The number one song on many a Christians'
"top ten" list these days is "He Touched Me." This is
a beautiful song and really expresses the truth that
God has made us whole people through Jesus Christ.
Unfortunately, however, there are times when the emphasis of the song seems to be "He touched *Me*." All
attention is focused on the singer or speaker. Look at

me! *My* life was once one high after another in sin. But *I* gave up that exciting life. (Almost tempting, isn't it?) The world really lost out when it lost *me*. Now *I'm* so different. Don't you wish you could be like *me*? Well, maybe it's not quite that bad, but you get the point. There's so much glory given to the messenger that the message is lost. When Jesus touched and healed the leper in Luke 5:12-14, the glory is placed where it belongs—on Christ.

Throughout the Bible leprosy is a picture of sin, and it is anything but exciting. God uses this horrible sickness to depict for us the ugliness of sin. Leprosy is a disease of the entire body. The man in Luke 5 was not a leper because he was covered with the ulcers and sores of leprosy. These were but external symptoms of the systemic disease. He was "full of leprosy" (verse 12). What a picture of mankind—you and me. The sins we commit are but surface symptoms of our true condition. We are sinners by nature—through and through!

Leprosy is a loathsome disease. It starts showing with only small blotches on the skin, but slowly and surely it eats away and disfigures the whole body. Fingers, toes, ears, nose are gradually lost. During biblical times there was no known cure for leprosy. It was only a matter of time before death overcame the victim. Could anything be more descriptive of sin and its result? At first, sin's ugliness may not be perceived. In fact, we can hide it under a variety of smart-looking "clothes" called facades. But before long its loathsome presence begins to show. Jealousy over a roommate's good grades or popularity; the silent treatment for a former friend; unwillingness to submit to a parent's authority; inability to yield to a boss's decision; all these are symptoms of the disease called sin. Apart from God there is no cure and sin continues to eat away and make life miserable. What about the pleasures of sin? It is the same thing. There may be excitement for a time, but slowly sin takes its toll. Our life style becomes selfish and sick. Our thought patterns become warped. We're disfigured. We're not whole. We have reaped what we have sown (Galatians 6:7). And eternal death is the sure result of sin. "For the wages of sin is death" (Romans 6:23).

Let us never forget to view sin the way God sees it: not exciting, but loathsome! Without the touch of God man is like the dying leper—not much of a prize! Remember, all glory is on God's side of the touch!

The hopeful request of the leper brought the healing touch of the Lord Jesus. The leper didn't doubt the Lord's ability but was afraid that Jesus might not be willing. "Lord, if you are willing, You can make me clean" (Luke 5:12). Sounds familiar, doesn't it? Many people never doubt the power and ability of God but think their cases are too far gone for God to want to help. No! The Lord Jesus will always say, "I am willing" (verse 13). There is no such thing as a person who is so involved in the ugliness of sin that Jesus turns away. Anyone who, like the leper, falls on his face (verse 12) and calls for mercy receives the healing touch of God Himself. And the cleansing is immediate (verse 13).

The fact that Jesus *touched* the leper is significant. Leprosy is a contagious disease and lepers had to live outside the city and call, "Unclean!" when anyone came near. The compassion of the Lord Jesus is seen as He reaches out and touches the open ulcers and sores of the disfigured leper. What a picture of God's love for us! Forever our song will be "*He* touched me!"

Verse 14 may need some explanation. The Lord was not interested in becoming a popular hero. Therefore He told the healed man to go quietly to the temple and show himself to the priest in accordance with the law of God as given to Moses in Leviticus 14. Jesus said that this action itself would be a testimony to the priests—those unbelieving priests of the religious establishment which would not accept the Lord. What a testimony! How could they doubt that Jesus was the Christ when they saw the change in this man? There may be a lesson here for us too. Let us spend more time in quiet obedience to our Savior. We can talk a good testimony but it is the consistent action of a changed life in obedience to the Word of God that will be the most effective testimony to those skeptics around us. They don't want to *hear* that "He touched *Me*." They need to *see* that "*He* touched me."

8

The Walls of Jericho

Hebrews 11:30 By faith the walls of Jericho fell down, after they had been encircled for seven days.

Just about everyone has heard the story of Joshua and the walls of Jericho. It's probably because of the song, "Joshua fit the battle of Jericho, and the walls come a-tumblin' down." In any case, the story is no legend or myth. About forty years after the Hebrews made their exodus from Egypt, they fought a decisive battle at Jericho in order to establish a beachhead in the new homeland. Jericho was a walled city and presented a major obstacle to the Hebrews because it was right in the middle of their path into the promised land. Jericho had to be eliminated. Because the Hebrews looked to the Lord in faith, God miraculously took Jericho out of their way and the conquest of the holy land was able to proceed.

The sixth chapter of the book of Joshua gives us the dramatic account of this unique battle in history.

Read Joshua chapters 1–6 in order to see all the important steps leading up to that climactic moment when the walls of Jericho collapsed. All of this is important history, because it is the divine record of how Israel received the land that God had promised them long before (Genesis 15:18). Through this nation in this land was to come the Savior for all mankind!

Besides the important history contained in the book of Joshua, there are some valuable spiritual lessons to be learned as well. There is the practical and devotional side to Joshua as well as the historical. The records of the battles that Israel fought contain spiritual principles for Christian warfare. We know from Scripture that we are involved in spiritual struggles with the enemy of our souls (Ephesians 6:11-17). Satan wants to keep us growing Christians from enjoying the spiritual blessings which are available to us in Christ. There really is love, joy, peace, rest, freedom, hope, security, intimate fellowship, and whatever else you long for to be experienced in the "promised land" of the Christian life. But Satan puts up his "Jerichos" to keep us "out of the land." The walls of doubt and discouragement and despair become major obstacles in the path of the Christian. A particular sin in the growing Christian's life can become a Jericho. The barriers seem insurmountable, and Satan laughs as we cringe in fear or are content to live "in the wilderness" of Christian experience. Are there any Jerichos in your life? The walls must fall!

Israel was God's earthly people. He gave them an earthly inheritance and promised them earthly blessings (Joshua 1:3). All they had to do was go in and possess the land (1:11). God did not want His people living in the wilderness any longer. They had been there for about forty years because of murmuring and complaining, disobedience, and unbelief. (See Numbers 32:13; 1 Corinthians 10:5-11; Hebrews 3:15-19.) Now they were to move out with renewed dedication and claim that good land—the land "flowing with milk and honey" (Exodus 3:8). The Lord promised them victory over Jericho and over the whole land. He also promised them His constant presence (Joshua 1:5). There was no need to be afraid or dismayed (1:9).

What a picture of the Christian life! We are God's people, and He has given us a heavenly inheritance and all kinds of spiritual blessings. We see from this picture that there are two possible reasons why we fail to enjoy the "milk and honey" of Christian living. Murmuring and complaining and unbelief are bound to result in "desert living." Failure to claim our "promised land" will lead to the same. We are not to wait till we get to heaven to enjoy our heavenly inheritance. God wants us to "cross the Jordan" and claim the blessings which we have in Christ right now. This is what Ephesians 1:3 means when it says, "Blessed be the God and Father of our Lord Jesus Christ, who has blessed us with every spiritual blessing in heavenly places in Christ." (See Ephesians 1:4-14 for a list of some of our spiritual blessings. Are you enjoying all these?) Yes, the good things of the "promised land" are ours for the taking, but we must claim them and appropriate them before we call them our own (Joshua 1:3). A Christian who is afraid to die has not really claimed his security in Christ. A Christian who is worried about his future has not really appropriated the peace which is available in Christ. A Christian who is always complaining and discontented has not really experienced the joy and peace of the kingdom. (See Romans 14:17.) A Christian who can never get along with his brothers and sisters in the Lord has not really walked in the land of overwhelming love which is available to every Christian. (See John 15:9 and think of how much love exists between Father and Son—that's how much is given to us!)

But what about those Jerichos? They are there because Satan knows that the frustrated Christian is an ineffective Christian. He also knows that the Christian who is enjoying the blessings of Christ is a Christian who is moving out and spreading the good news of the kingdom of God. Therefore Satan will do anything in his power to keep us defeated and scared and "throwing in the towel." But God has promised us victory (Romans 8:37) just as He promised Joshua. He has also promised us His constant personal presence (Hebrews 13:5) just as He promised Joshua. There is no need to fear (2 Timothy 1:7). There are no Jericho walls that are too high or too thick for our God. What is the Jericho that is keeping you from fully entering the "land of blessing" that God has in store for you? The walls of doubt or fear or temptation or a secret sin are not impregnable!

Victory over Jericho was guaranteed, but it was not automatic. Israel had to follow the instructions that God had given them to be sure of victory. We too must follow the instructions that God has given us if we are to see the "walls come tumbling down." In the steps leading up to the fall of Jericho we see some spiritual principles which, when applied, bring sure victory. The first and foremost principle is to know and obey and apply the Word of God (Joshua 1:7-8). The "law" here means the first five books of the Bible—the only Scriptures that the people had at that time. We must do more than "get a little Bible" each week. We must study God's Word until it is such a part of us that it characterizes our talk (verse 8). We must obey it without compromising (verse 7). We must obey all that is written (verse 8). Then and only then will we be successful (verses 7-8). This is the secret of success for the Christian.

Another principle for victory which emerges from these early chapters of Joshua is to "follow the ark." Now this principle will sound farfetched until we realize that God is painting a picture here in the Scriptures to illustrate the principle He wants us to learn. The ark mentioned in Joshua 3 and 4 was not some big boat like Noah's ark; it was a trunk-sized sacred box that the priests carried as the Hebrews journeyed from Egypt to the promised land. The ark was kept in the most holy place of Israel's tent of worship. (They didn't have a temple until years later under King Solomon.) The ark represented the meeting place between God and man. Once a year the blood of the Old Testament sacrifices had to be presented on the ark before the Lord. It was this ark that opened up the way through the Jordan River into the promised land (Joshua 3:13-17). It was this ark that was carried in the midst of the Hebrew people when they marched around Jericho (Joshua 6:8-9). Now in the illustration that God has drawn for us, the ark pictures the Lord Jesus. He is the meeting place between God and man. (See John 14:6 and 1 Timothy 2:5.) He is the One whose blood was presented once and for all before God to settle the problem of sin (Hebrews 9:11-15). He is the One who opened up the way into the "land of blessing." He is the One who must be at the center of our march of faith around those Jerichos in our lives. Our walk of faith must be Christ-centered if the walls are to fall!

There are many other spiritual principles of victory contained in the book of Joshua, but these two "biggies" are enough to get you "into the land" where you will start to enjoy your inheritance in Christ. If we put Christ where He belongs in our lives and absorb His Word until it characterizes our lives, there will be no room for those Jericho obstacles. Those barrier walls will just disappear. The Jerichos in your life may take a little time to fall—remember, the walls did not fall until the people encircled the city by faith for seven days. But if the principles are really applied (no shortcuts!) the walls cannot remain. The walls of Jericho *will* fall down!

9

Far-out Wisdom

James 1:5   But if any of you lacks wisdom,
let him ask of God, who gives to all men
generously and without reproach, and it will
be given to him.
James 3:13-17   Who among you is wise
and understanding? Let him show by his good
behavior his deeds in the gentleness of
wisdom. But if you have bitter jealousy and
selfish ambition in your heart, do not be
arrogant and so lie against the truth. This
wisdom is not that which comes down from
above, but is earthly, natural, demonic. For
where jealousy and selfish ambition exist,
there is disorder and every evil thing. But the
wisdom from above is first pure, then
peaceable, gentle, reasonable, full of mercy
and good fruits, unwavering, without
hypocrisy.

The Lord told me that I'm to marry you," a
persistent Christian guy told his Christian girlfriend.
"Well, He hasn't given me the same instructions," re-

plied the confused girl. Maybe you have never been involved in a situation quite like this, but surely you have often been faced with a decision to make and are confused as to the right answer. You've even prayed about the matter but still there's no "burst of light" or "voice from the sky." You may have some slight feeling that God has already given you the answer but you can't be sure. Does the Lord send specific answers? How can a Christian know for sure when he has the Lord's answer?

Our Scriptures tell us that there is wisdom from God which is definitely available to the Christian upon request. This wisdom is not our own natural "smarts" but is wisdom from above—all the way from heaven— "far-out wisdom!" However, this wisdom is not easily or automatically obtained. These Scriptures give us two reasons why. First, the wisdom from God is an answer to prayer (James 1:5). This puts us right in the middle of an arena of conflict. The wisdom of God comes to prayer warriors across a spiritual battlefield. And answers to prayer are louder and clearer to those in the front lines. As one moves away from the battle zone the sound becomes less distinct—and ears less trained! The answers are barely heard back in the "rest and relaxation" zones. We must persevere in prayer. (Read Ephesians 6:11-18 and note especially verse 18.) Second, there is another wisdom that shouts to be heard (James 3:15). This wisdom is not from above but it is the wisdom of this world ("earthly"), which is no higher than man's fallen and sinful mind ("natural"), and is even influenced by Satan himself ("demonic"). Which wisdom are you hearing?

Amidst the conflict and the clamor are there any clues given to help us detect the wisdom from above which we are seeking? Yes, there are both subjective and objective clues. Subjective clues have reference to our own motives. Verses 14 and 15 indicate that if there is any jealousy or selfish ambition involved on our part, then it cannot be the wisdom from God. The voice which says, "Defend your own rights at all costs!" is not the voice of God. The Christian who has wisdom from above is willing to be wronged and defrauded (1 Corinthians 6:7) rather than defend his own personal rights and interests. Far-out indeed! James 3:13 (KJV) says the same thing in a positive way. The wise Christian is meek! The word "meekness" in the Bible does not convey the idea of weakness or no backbone or "pushover" or Mr. Milquetoast! Meek has to do with inner attitudes rather than outward actions. It is the opposite of *self*-assertiveness and *self*-interest. Our Lord was meek (Matthew, 11:29, KJV). Consider His words and actions concerning His own personal rights during that mockery of a trial before His crucifixion! If we are characterized by meekness we will be in tune with the wisdom from above which God longs to share with us. But if the "Big I" is on the throne of our lives, then forget it! We will not only miss out on the answers from above, but, as verse 16 indicates, our lives will be characterized by disorder and worthless activities. In fact, a person so characterized should not even expect an answer from heaven (James 1:6-8).

Objectively, the wisdom from above is clearly defined in James 3:17. It is *first* of all *pure*. The Lord never asks us to do anything shady or under the table. Calling in sick to work in order to have time off to attend a Christian retreat is definitely not God's answer to prayer!

Wisdom from above is *peaceable*. It never seeks to settle matters by "rocking the boat"—if at all possible.

Wisdom from above is *gentle*. God's wisdom is always considerate and tender. It is just, but tempered with mercy. In other words, my answer to prayer about whether or not to offer assistance to a person in need will more than likely be "Go the second mile!" (Matthew 5:41).

Wisdom from above is *reasonable*. A pharisaical attitude of, "I've got the last word and you must agree with me," definitely smacks of wisdom from below. A Christian following wisdom from above is not stubborn-minded, narrow-minded, or closed-minded.

Wisdom from above is *full of mercy and good fruits*. Our fellow students and neighbors are trapped and struggling in the vortex of this doomed, sin-sick world. When we are aligned with God's wisdom we not only *feel* pity ("mercy") for those in need, but we *do* something ("good fruits") to help them.

Wisdom from above is *unwavering*. When God shares His wisdom with us in answer to our earnest prayers, there is no uncertainty or inconsistency about it. We can move out with confidence because we know we have the mind of God.

Wisdom from above is *without hypocrisy*. This should be so obvious, yet how we fool ourselves into thinking we are walking in the wisdom from above while all along we are doing our own thing and just playacting as "Joe Christian."

One last thought: if we want to be extra sure that we are in line with wisdom from above, then let us go all out to follow the Lord Jesus because "in [Him] are hidden all the treasures of wisdom and knowledge"

(Colossians 2:3). Then we can say for *sure* "we have the mind of Christ" (1 Corinthians 2:16). Far-out, but true!

10

Spiritual Leadership

Ezra 7:10   For Ezra had set his heart to
study the law of the LORD, and to practice it,
and to teach His statutes and ordinances in
Israel.
Read all of Ezra 7–10.

Spiritual leadership is not the same as military
leadership, political leadership, or corporate leadership. This is not to say that there are no similarities
between spiritual leadership and these other kinds of
leadership. There are certain elements common to all
types of leadership. Furthermore, the good qualities of
military leadership, political leadership, or corporate
leadership can certainly be used by the Lord when a
committed Christian dedicates these natural and developed abilities to Christ. Spiritual leadership, however, is more than just dedicated natural traits and
talents. Successful Christian businesspersons, for example, do not necessarily have what it takes to be successful spiritual leaders. They may be very effective in

leading a company or a campus organization, but this is no guarantee that they will be effective leaders in a church or ministry, even though they may be dynamic Christians. The reason for this is that there is an added dimension to spiritual leadership; it requires more than dedicated natural abilities. Spiritual leadership, simply defined, is God-given spiritual ability and responsibility to lead God's people. This all-important dimension is a must for effective leadership in any Christian service. Let's be careful not to read our own cultural concepts of successful leadership into the biblical standards when we're choosing or recognizing our spiritual leaders.

There are many examples of spiritual leaders in the Bible. Ezra of the Old Testament is an outstanding example. In chapters 7 through 10 of the little book of Scripture that bears his name, we learn that Ezra not only fully dedicated his natural abilities and talents to the service of the Lord, but he also had that added ingredient of spiritual ability and responsibility for leading God's people. In fact, of the three post-exilic leaders of the Jewish people, Ezra is remembered most for his spiritual leadership. Zerubbabel is remembered for leading the people in the reconstruction of the temple; Nehemiah is remembered for leading the people in the rebuilding of the wall of Jerusalem; Ezra is remembered for leading the people in spiritual revival. As we look at the inspired record of Ezra's leadership in these chapters, we can gain a great deal of insight into the kind of people God uses as spiritual leaders.

First and foremost, we see that Ezra was a person who was devoted to God's Word. His priestly background and training (Ezra 7:1-5) certainly contributed to this, but Ezra had gone further in his devotion to the Word of God; he had become a scribe. The Hebrew scribes of that day not only copied the ancient sacred scrolls; they studied and taught these Scriptures as well. Ezra's devotion to the Word can almost be felt in Ezra 7:10. Ezra had set his heart to study and practice and teach the law of the Lord. No wonder he was skilled (verse 6) in the application of the Scripture to life's situations. This is the kind of spiritual leadership that is needed today. God is looking for Christians who are devoted to studying His Word and to practicing and applying the principles for Christian living that it contains. Becoming skillful in the use and application of God's Word takes more than a Sunday school background and a brief quiet time each day. There must be that devoted heart—set on the study of the law of the Lord. Could God choose you right now as a spiritual leader?

Ezra was also a man of prayer. He practiced what we all preach but something we do so seldom. Ezra prayed about everything. He prayed for a safe journey before the long trip from Babylon to Jerusalem. In his prayer he included the children and even their material possessions (Ezra 8:21). Yes, it is biblical to pray for safety on the road before a long trip. But Ezra prayed about more than just the mundane things of everyday living. When he heard the sad news about the moral condition of God's people living in Judah, Ezra prayed a long prayer of confession (Ezra 9:5-15). Although Ezra himself was not guilty, he humbly identified with the nation in their sin. He poured out his soul before God on behalf of the people. His prayer life was not self-centered. Ezra was characterized by a heart for the people of God. This is the kind of person the Lord chooses for spiritual leadership. Do we qualify? Notice

how Ezra's example led the people to repentance (Ezra
10:1). Spiritual leaders with an Ezra-like prayer life
will find similar results today.

Ezra knew how to work well with people. This was
another very important and necessary aspect of his
God-given ability as a spiritual leader. He could motivate people to move in the right direction without
manipulating them. For example, when no Levites
showed up to go back to Jerusalem (Ezra 8:15), Ezra
used just the right approach to get a number of Levites
to change their minds. This was no easy task. Joining
the caravan meant saying goodbye to relatives, business, property, and the easy life in Babylon, and taking
the long trip to Jerusalem—a city still much in ruins
from Nebuchadnezzar's invasion over one hundred
years before. And the Levites had no prospect of strik-
ing it rich back in Jerusalem. No, they would be required to get involved in the unglamorous work of the
temple. Remember, they were the tribe of Israel which
was responsible for helping the priests with all the necessary legwork around the house of the Lord. Why
would any Levite want to leave the good life in Babylon
for that? But somehow Ezra was able to motivate over
two hundred-fifty of the Levites to leave their prosperous life in Babylon for the service of the house of
the Lord in Jerusalem. That took God-given spiritual
ability. Spiritual leadership like that is needed today to
motivate Christians to get going, especially in the
humdrum, everyday areas of Christian service.

Another evidence of Ezra's ability to work well with
people was his flexible firmness. This sounds like a
contradiction in terms, but it really isn't. When Ezra
was confronted with a moral problem on the part of
God's people (Ezra 9:1-4), he didn't condone sin or

change God's standards to water down the problem. He remained firm in his position that the people had greatly sinned before God and that serious action must be taken. At the same time, however, Ezra was flexible in the way he went about handling the problem. He was willing to take helpful advice from Shecaniah (Ezra 10:2-4). Some would-be spiritual leaders today would never take advice from their flock. They are inflexible in their ideas of what is to be done and how it is to be done. They need to take a lesson from Ezra on flexibility.

Ezra's flexible firmness is further observed when the people assembled in the open square in Jerusalem (Ezra 10:9). His firmness is shown in his continual support of biblical standards and the necessity of getting the problem of intermarriage with the pagans resolved (verses 10-11). His flexibility is seen in his willingness to listen to reason (verses 12-15). The people admitted their guilt and they really wanted to set things straight, but they needed a little more time. Besides, it was raining and they were getting chilled. Ezra wasn't so rigid a leader that he demanded the matter be settled immediately, rain or no rain. Unfortunately, some Christian leaders today are that rigid. They are inflexible and demanding and will not listen to reason. Consequently, they do not work well with people and therefore cannot possibly be good spiritual leaders. Ezra knew that the people were repentant in heart and were not just stalling for time. He was therefore confident that the matter would be corrected in good time—and it was (verses 16-19).

Ezra's handling of money is one more important indication of his spiritual leadership. This is a critical area, and many spiritual leaders since Ezra's time have failed because of mistakes in the matter of money. Notice how Ezra avoided two dangerous extremes. On the one hand, he made sure that he did not allow himself to get too close to the money, where he could easily be tempted or accused of mismanagement. He delegated the responsibility for looking after the funds to twelve reliable men (Ezra 8:24-30). These funds included freewill offerings from God's people in Babylon as well as monies from the royal treasury of the Persian king, Artaxerxes (Ezra 7:11-20). I wonder if we could have kept our hands off the cash if the offer of Ezra 7:18 had been made to us. What purchases for our own selfish interests and desires would we have condoned? As a spiritual leader, Ezra avoided those potential problems by releasing direct control over the treasury.

On the other hand, Ezra avoided the extreme of divorcing himself completely from the financial end of things. He made sure that the money was not only in good hands, but that everything was completely accounted for (Ezra 8:33-34). Spiritual leaders must keep tabs on what's being done with the funds entrusted to them. Practically speaking, there is a financial side to every Christian church and ministry, and the proper use of money is a spiritual matter. Avoiding the two extremes can be difficult at times, but a balanced approach to finances is a mark of a good spiritual leader.

Several times over in these chapters from the book of Ezra we are told that the good hand of God was upon Ezra. (See Ezra 7:6,9,28; 8:18,22,31.) God never calls people to spiritual leadership without also giving them the necessary ability to do the job. Because spiritual leadership is a God-given ability and responsibility to lead His people, you can be sure that if you are ever called to such a role, the good hand of God will be available to you.

11

Return of a Rebel

Luke 15:17-20, NIV   When he came to his
senses, he said, How many of my father's
hired men have food to spare, and here I am
starving to death! I will set out and go back
to my father and say to him: Father, I have
sinned against heaven and against you. I am
no longer worthy to be called your son; make
me like one of your hired men. So he got up
and went to his father.
Read the entire story in Luke 15:11-32.

Have you ever tried to run away? Probably
most of us have had the desire, at least, to run at one
time or another. If we could just get away from our
duties and responsibilities at home. If we could just
leave our problems and some of those tense personal
relationships. If we could just terminate our associations with all those "superiors" who are always telling
us what to do.

In a very practical way the story of the runaway son
in Luke 15 shows us that running away does not pay.

The life of the rebel is never really free. Running away from responsibilities and problems and authority brings only short-lived freedom, and invariably results in more frustration than before (verses 13-16). Real freedom only comes when we begin to deal with the root cause of our desire to run away (verses 17-18). The root cause of our problem is always related to our relationship with God. We run because we are unwilling to submit to an authority or handle the responsibilities that God has placed in our lives. We run because we refuse to admit that many of our "problems" are not the fault of others, but are the results of our own selfish desires. We must return in repentance and confess our rebellious actions to the Lord (verses 20-21). It is the returned and repentant rebel who, paradoxically, finds the freedom and happiness and love he was looking for all along (verses 22-24).

The story goes on (verses 25-31) to show that it is not only *open* rebellious *actions* which bring unhappiness and frustration and separation. In the older son we see *hidden* rebellious *attitudes*. The older son did not run away, but he was a rebel at heart. His open bitterness and bad attitude were but surface symptoms of the restless and rebellious spirit within. There must be repentance of hidden attitudes as well as of obvious actions if we are to know and experience joy and communion with the Father.

There is much more that we can learn from this story of the two sons. Like many of the other parables of our Lord Jesus, the story had a primary application to the people then, but contains valuable spiritual lessons which apply to us today. Notice that the parable was given in the presence of the tax collectors and sinners, as well as the Pharisees and the scribes (verses

1-2). The tax collectors and "sinners" openly recognized their shortcomings and they gladly heard the Lord. The Pharisees and scribes, on the other hand, were self-righteous, religious people who resented the fact that Jesus was the friend of unclean people like lepers and social outcasts—He even ate with them (verse 2)!

In Luke 15 the Lord Jesus gave three parables (the lost sheep, the lost coin, and the lost son) to show that the hypocritical scribes and Pharisees needed to repent and admit that they were as lost as the "open" sinners. Thus the primary teaching of the story of the two sons was directed at the self-righteous religious leaders. They are pictured in the older son as rebellious (verse 28), self-righteous (verse 29), jealous (verse 30), and unthankful for the privileged place in which God had placed the Jewish nation (verse 31).

In the parable, the runaway son is a picture of the tax collectors and open sinners in the crowd. Tax collectors were Jews who made their living by collecting taxes for Rome. Usually they collected more than Rome demanded and pocketed the difference. Thus they were considered extortioners and collaborators with the enemy by their own people. Notice that in no way does the Lord condone their sin. The lost and sinful condition of the tax collectors is pictured as an empty and wasted life far from God (verses 13-16). (Nothing could be more repulsive for a Jew than to work for a foreign Gentile, caring for his pigs.) But many of these rebels "came to their senses" (verse 17) when they heard the message of the Lord Jesus. They willingly acknowledged their unworthiness and repented of their sins (verses 18-19). The amazing and wonderful truth that Jesus proclaimed to His listeners

is that God does not take back returned rebels reluc-
tantly—He welcomes them with open arms and celebration (verses 20-24). The cutting edge of the
parable is that the repentant, traitorous tax collectors
and the repentant, sinful, common people were
brought into an intimate and happy relationship with
God, while the self-righteous and religious scribes and
Pharisees of respectable society were "left out in the
cold"! The teaching of the Lord Jesus was clear and to
the point—it is not religion, but repentance that
counts with God!

The story of the two sons certainly has some things
to say to us today. In the description of both sons there
is a wealth of teaching. One doesn't have to look very
far today to find the older brother of the story—he
can even be found in the church. This is the respectable, self-righteous religious person who thinks he or
she is chalking up points with God, and that because
of this, God owes him something (verse 29). He has
never involved himself in drugs or sex sin or robbery
or wasted time like some others whom he is quick to
point out and accuse (verse 30). He is angry and jealous when he finds out that others are actually enjoying
a relationship with God (verses 25-28). The older
brother of today doesn't really care about his brothers.
Notice how he does not say "my brother" in verse 30,
but rather he says "your son." The older brother's attitude is always, "Let them get what they deserve!"
Grace and mercy and love are words which a self-
righteous person does not understand. How could he?
He has no real love for God. It's only "what's in it for
me?" that matters. That's why the older brother in the
story stuck around home—for the property, not out
of love for the father. Notice that the older son never

says "father" in the story. Notice, also, how he accuses
the father of favoritism because he hadn't given him
a party for himself and his friends. He didn't care at
all about his relationship with his father (verse 29)!
The respectable, self-righteous religious person is also
a rebel at heart.

In the runaway son we have a picture of ourselves
before conversion, running away and rebelling against
God. God, our Creator, pictured here as the kind
Father, gives us life and other "property" to use intel-
ligently and for His glory. Some people are given more
than others, but no one can say that he hasn't been
given a "share of the estate" (verse 12). But we live
for ourselves and squander the precious time and talents that God has given us (verse 13). We don't want
to be subject to God. We'd rather "get what's ours"
and enjoy ourselves in our own way in the "far country"—as far away from God as we can get. The far
country in verse 13 can be quite close to home; the
distance is measured in motives, not miles.

There comes a time in the rebel's life when the
runnings stops. With the knowledge of emptiness and
hunger in our souls comes the realization of how
wretched we really are (verse 14). It is hard to admit
that we are not the "big independent spenders" we
once thought we were; rather, we are living like dirty,
smelly pigs (verse 15)! And the empty "husks" of the
far country do not really fill the emptiness within us
(verse 16). There is no real freedom or satisfaction for
the soul of man apart from total surrender to God and
communion with Him.

The return of every rebel begins with repentance.
As rebels against God, we must realize that we are
separated from Him and dying because of our sin

(verse 17); we are also the "lost" and "dead" of verse 24. We must confess: "Oh God, I have sinned" (verse 18). We must admit that God owes us nothing and that we have no claims on God (verse 19).

Up to this point God is seen as longing for our return but not forcing Himself on us. But notice the action of the Father when, by an act of our will, we "get up" and begin our return (verse 20). The Lord has been watching and waiting for us all along, and now He actually runs to us and smothers us with affection! What a picture of the love God has for you and me!

Why is there no reprimand? Why is there no scolding? The father is so overjoyed (note verse 7 also) that the son never even gets to finish his formal confession (compare verse 21 with verses 18 and 19). The repentant son is given the best robe (this signified a position of honor in those days), a ring (this was a sign of authority), and sandals (this was for family members only—slaves were not given shoes). Not only is everything forgiven, but there is complete reconciliation between father and son. Why? Because it is a picture of God's tremendous love and unbelievable plan of salvation for us. When we turn back to God, our sins are completely forgiven and we are brought into a favored position in the family of God—with no strings attached! Our salvation is far more than a "ticket to heaven" or "fire insurance." And the celebration has just begun (verses 23-24)!

Although there are no strings attached for us, it cost God a great price to bring us back into fellowship with Himself: the death of His beloved Son, the Lord Jesus. In John 14:6, Acts 4:12, and 1 Timothy 2:5 we see that the return path of the rebel must be through

Jesus Christ. It is through His death for us that our rebellious actions and attitudes are forgiven, our place in God's family is restored, and a never ending celebration and communion with God begun.

12

Strong but Weak

Judges 16:21   Then the Philistines seized [Samson] and gouged out his eyes; and they brought him down to Gaza and bound him with bronze chains, and he was a grinder in the prison.
Read the story of Samson in Judges 13–16.

What man ripped apart an attacking lion with his bare hands? What individual, singlehandedly, killed one thousand of the enemy in battle with only the jawbone of a donkey as a weapon? What weight lifter pressed the doors and posts of an ancient city gate weighing at least one thousand pounds, and then put the whole thing on his shoulders and carried it for about thirty-eight miles uphill to the top of a mountain? What "demolition expert" pushed down a large house with just one mighty thrust of his arms? It sounds like the "Six Million Dollar Man." Wrong! Then it must be the new Superman! Wrong again! The answer, of course, to these "Ripley's Believe It or Not" questions is not some make-believe creation of TV or the movies but the real life Samson of the Bible.

The Bible has quite a bit to say about Samson. Four whole chapters are devoted to a character study of this strong man. Everyone tends to remember what the Bible says about Samson's strength, but the biblical record tells us a lot more about this leader of ancient Israel. The story of Samson is a study in contrasts. We see the tremendous feats of Samson's physical strength on the one hand and his obvious spiritual shortcomings on the other. He was strong but weak! God has included in His Word this account about Samson, not just that we may stand in awe at the strength of the world's strongest man, but that we may learn the lessons for growing Christians that are recorded here. (See Romans 15:4.)

Samson lived in Israel during the period of the judges. In fact, Samson was the last judge of Israel before Samuel. Soon after Samson's death, Saul was anointed by Samuel as the first king of Israel. The period of the judges was certainly not a time of spiritual growth in Israel's history. The people of Israel had degenerated since the days of Moses and Joshua. Disobedience to the Word of the Lord was the reason for this downhill spiral. A do-your-own-thing attitude characterized the age of judges. Judges 17:6 and 21:25 state that "everyone did that which was right in his own eyes." God permitted the enemies of Israel to come in and oppress and defeat His people because of their sin. Periodically during these dark days, the people of Israel cried out to the Lord for help. God then graciously raised up a judge to deliver them. But soon after they were delivered, they turned their backs on the Lord again and plunged into renewed idolatry and immorality.

Against such a background Samson came on the scene. It was during a time of Philistine oppression. Right from the start Samson had everything going for him. If ever there was a candidate most likely to succeed, young Samson was that person. In chapter 13 we learn that Samson came from a solid home. He had godly parents who believed and worshiped the Lord. Furthermore, Samson was designated by God Himself to be a deliverer of Israel from the hands of the Philistines (Judges 13:5). Victory was guaranteed. What more could one ask for? And then, of course, there was Samson's physique. Not only did God bless him with great physical strength but it seems that God gave him good looks as well. (An ugly Samson just could not have had the success that Samson had with the Philistine women!) On top of all this, we read further that God blessed young Samson and the Spirit of the Lord was at work in his life (13:24-25). What a tremendous foundation on which to build! What potential! In light of such a beginning, how sad it is to read the above Scripture (16:21) concerning Samson's tragic end: gouged-out eyes, bound with chains, harnessed like an ox, imprisoned by the Philistines. Instead of delivering Israel from the Philistines, Samson had delivered himself to the enemy. Who would have ever believed that this could happen to Samson, the teenager who had everything going for him? What went wrong, anyway?

It doesn't take much insight to discover the key to Samson's downfall. It is found over and over again in chapters 14 through 16. Samson had no self-control.

He could not govern his passions. He was weak-willed and self-willed. What he wanted, he wanted now. "Not Thy will but mine be done" was Samson's standard operating procedure. Look, for example, at Samson's uncontrolled selfish passion in chapter 14:1-4. He saw a beautiful pagan Philistine woman and wanted her. His selfish response to the godly counsel of his parents was, "Get her for me, for she looks good to me." Decisions made only on the basis of looks and pleasure are usually a sign of little self-control. How are your decisions made? Look also at Samson's weakness with Delilah in chapter 16. Because of his selfish "love" for this ungodly Philistine woman, Samson not only gave her the secret of his strength but he sold her his soul as well; "he told her all that was in his heart" (verse 17). The almost unbelievable magnitude of Samson's weakness is seen only when it is realized that he had three clear warnings of what was coming (verses 8-14). How blind could Samson be, especially when Delilah had told him openly why she wanted to know his secret. "Please tell me where your great strength is and how you may be bound to afflict you" (verse 6). How important it is for a growing Christian not to fall in love with an unbeliever. Love can be so blind at times that you do things you never dreamed possible, against all logic and common sense. What a mess you can get yourself into if you fall in love with a "Delilah." No wonder God's Word says that marriage between believers and unbelievers is wrong. (See 2 Corinthians 6:14.)

Step by step Samson let his lack of self-control take over. He had taken the Nazarite vow as a youth, but one by one he was breaking the rules because of his undisciplined and selfish life. There were several standards or rules to be kept by the Nazarite (no connection with the word Nazarene): no drinking of wine or strong drink, no eating of anything produced by the grapevine, no cutting of hair, no touching of dead bodies, no mixing with anything which would affect his separation unto the Lord. (See Numbers 6.) Now follow Samson's life and you will see how he broke every one of the rules because of his uncontrolled selfish desires. The vineyards of Timnah (Judges 14:5) in Philistia were the last place Samson should have been— let alone marrying a Philistine, which was against God's command for any Hebrew. (See Deuteronomy 7:1-6.) Then Samson defiled himself by touching the carcass of the dead lion (Judges 14:8-9). Instead of taking the necessary steps for cleansing, Samson made light of his violation by making it part of a riddle (verse 14). And where did Samson present his riddle? At a feast for Philistines, where strong drink was certainly part of the custom (verse 10). At the beginning of chapter 16 we see Samson making love with not just a Philistine, but with a Philistine prostitute. Uncontrolled passion took priority over Nazarite vows. And finally there was Delilah and the Philistine razor.

But what about Samson's great feats of strength against the Philistines? Even here we find Samson using his God-given supernatural strength for his own ends. Trace the record of Samson's mighty displays of strength and you will find that in every case Samson's motive was basically selfish and not for the glory of God or the deliverance of Israel. Even at the end, when the Lord granted Samson his last request (Judges 16:28-30), we note that there is no record of repentance on Samson's part. There is only a somewhat selfish request, "that I may be avenged of the Philistines for my two eyes."

There is a powerful lesson for growing Christians in all of this. We too may have a lot of God-given potential, but we may also utterly fail because of no self-control. Like Samson, we may come from a solid Christian background where we have been taught the precepts and principles of the Word of God. But like Samson, we may turn our backs on the clear teaching of God's Word because we want to do our own thing and go our own way. Like Samson, we may have it all together in the physical area: good looks, talent, etc. But like Samson, we may take our God-given looks and talents and use them to indulge in selfish pleasure and passion. Even our spiritual gifts can be misused and abused because of selfish interests and ambitions. Without self-control, a growing Christian with great potential strength will be as weak as Samson. Control of our selfish desires and drives is extremely important and necessary in the Christian life. 2 Peter 1:5-7 tells us to use all diligence to add self-control to our faith. Galatians 5:16-23 assures us that more self-control is available for us and is given to those who make the things of God their top priority. Do you need more self-control? How are your priorities?

In spite of Samson's lack of self-control, God was still working with him and through him (see Judges 14:4,19; 15:14). And Hebrews 11:32 assures us that Samson had faith. All of this should be an encouragement to us who, so often, follow our own selfish desires, as Samson did. God can still accomplish His purposes through us, but how much greater to be yielded to His control and realize our full potential.

13

Models for the Faithful Christian

2 Timothy 2:3-6   Suffer hardship with me, as a good soldier of Christ Jesus. No soldier in active service entangles himself in the affairs of everyday life, so that he may please the one who enlisted him as a soldier. And also if any one competes as an athlete, he does not win the prize unless he competes according to the rules. The hard-working farmer ought to be the first to receive his share of the crops.

Second Timothy is the last correspondence we have from the apostle Paul; it was written to Timothy around A.D.66. The Roman persecutions of the early Christians had already started. The pagan emperor Nero had blamed the Christians for the great fire in Rome in A.D.64, and he used this as an excuse to throw many of them to the beasts in the Roman arena. It is recorded that Nero even used some Christians as human torches to light a sporting event in the imperial gardens. At this time Paul was imprisoned and awaiting his sentence of death (2 Timothy 4:6-7). From a dungeon in Rome, Paul penned this last letter to Timothy, his faithful and "beloved son" in the faith (2 Timothy 1:2 and Philippians 2:19-22).

Timothy had been brought to the Lord through the ministry of Paul about twenty years prior to this time—most likely when Timothy was a teenager. Since that time, a beautiful spiritual father-son relationship had developed between Paul and Timothy. Paul had taught young Timothy the great doctrines of the Christian faith. Timothy had accompanied Paul on his missionary journeys. Faithful Timothy didn't fail in the face of hardship and persecution. He didn't give up when Paul was imprisoned for a couple of years in Caesarea (A.D.58–60; Acts 23–26). He didn't desert when Paul was shipped as a prisoner to Rome. Timothy stayed close to his spiritual father while Paul remained under arrest for another couple of years in Rome (A.D.61–63; Acts 27–28).

It is almost certain that Paul was released from this first Roman imprisonment and that he continued his missionary travels for a few more years (A.D.63–65). Timothy went along as one of Paul's faithful fellow workers. Some time before Paul's rearrest by Roman authorities, Timothy was delegated by the apostle to remain at Ephesus to help pastor the church there. It may have been the tearful parting between Paul and Timothy at this time which is mentioned in 2 Timothy 1:4. Paul moved on in his travels, and as a faithful father he wrote back to Timothy with instructions and encouragement (the letter of 1 Timothy). The apostle continued to boldly proclaim wherever he went throughout the pagan Roman Empire the good news that Jesus Christ (not Caesar!) was Lord. Of course it wasn't long before Paul was rearrested and sent back to Rome. Chained as a criminal, he was placed in the dungeon to await his trial (2 Timothy 1:16 and 2:9). There in that cold and lonely cell Paul longed to see his faithful son Timothy again before he died (2 Timothy 1:4 and 4:9). We do not know whether Timothy made it to Rome before Paul was martyred. Reliable tradition indicates that soon after Paul wrote 2 Timothy he was executed at Rome—beheaded for his faith in Jesus Christ.

During those last days in prison Paul reflected on the rough road ahead for the young Christian church. Not only was there going to be more physical persecution from without, but there would also be spiritual declension from within (2 Timothy 3). Already many had turned away from the full message that Paul preached (2 Timothy 1:15). With this prophetic insight, Paul wrote this last letter to his spiritual son and encouraged him to remain steadfast in the faith. In spite of the impending persecution and heresy, Timothy was to "preach the word" and "fulfill his ministry" (2 Timothy 4:1-5). Paul was concerned that the pure and complete gospel of Jesus Christ be carried on, without changes or "watering down," by faithful Christians like Timothy (2 Timothy 1:13-14 and 2:1-2). In order to drive home the point of Timothy's crucial responsibility, Paul gave his son several models to follow. These models of the faithful Christian are found in 2 Timothy 2.

Before proceeding to the models, let us look at the valuable and practical lesson of the father-son relationship between Paul and Timothy. Growing Christians need "Pauls" and "Timothys." Paul-Timothy relationships are helpful and biblical. Is there a "Paul" or two in your life? If not, find an older and more mature Christian who would be willing to be a Paul to you: counsel you, teach you, write to you, and pray consistently for you (2 Timothy 1:3). And what about your "Timothys"? Do you have one or two younger Christians whom you are bringing along in the faith? God has given you the unique privilege (and awesome responsibility) of being the spiritual father or mother to that younger Christian in your school or dorm or neighborhood or church.

In 2 Timothy 2:3-6 we find three models for the growing Christian to follow: the soldier, the athlete, and the farmer. Each of these models shows us a particular aspect of the life of the faithful Christian that we are to follow. God did not put these models haphazardly into His Word for "local color"! Each model is there to show us something that God expects to see in the life of the growing Christian.

The key idea in the model of the soldier (verses 3-4) is *sacrifice*. The soldier here is not the American soldier who "joins the army to see the world," but rather the Roman soldier who sacrificed all to please the Emperor. The good soldier sacrificed the easy life (verse 3) and the secure life (verse 4a) and the independent life (verse 4b). Paul had certainly measured up to this model throughout his life of sacrificial service for the Lord Jesus. Now soldier Timothy is encouraged to do the same. And God expects to see some sacrifice in the life of every growing Christian. He has given us this model not just to admire, but to follow. A life of ease and security and independence must go if we are to be good soldiers of Jesus Christ. The faith-

ful Christian must sacrifice some of his free time and
fun time and "easy life" time. Unsacrificed large bank
accounts and worldly careers may bring earthly security, but they are the mark of questionable soldiers
in the Lord's army. A good soldier does not "do his
own thing," but sacrifices his independence and sub-
mits in obedience to his commanding officer. Are we
soldiers who are willing to sacrifice?

The model of the athlete is found in verse 5. The
particular athlete in view here is the Greek marathon
runner. A life of discipline was required as this athlete
trained for the Greek games (forerunner of today's
Olympic Games). Hours and hours of running and a
disciplined lifestyle were demanded if the athlete was
to be a winner. The serious athlete today knows what
disciplined training is all about. The application to the
growing Christian is obvious. We must be disciplined
in our training in the Christian life. Training rules may
include getting out of bed early each day to read God's
Word and pray. Determination to memorize Scripture
and to share our faith with non-Christians also involves healthy discipline. Many of us are "out of shape"
because of no discipline in our training.

The athlete must not only be disciplined in training
but also disciplined in running. He must compete according to the rules of the race as well as keep the
training rules. Imagine a Greek runner on his way into
the crowd filled stadium to complete the last few laps
of the long marathon run. As he comes to the final
turn of the last lap he is still twenty-five yards behind
the lead runner. He realizes he can't overtake him, so
he cuts across the field to the finish line. But no prize!
The wreath must go to the disciplined runner. How
true this is in the Christian life. What good is my

Christian testimony on campus if I cheat on exams? What kind of Christian am I if I conveniently "forget" to pay back some money, or keep the money from a store that mistakenly undercharged me? What good is my disciplined life of memorizing a verse a day if I am not disciplined in the way I "play the game"? God expects me to be like the athlete who wins the prize— disciplined in training and disciplined in running!

Another model that Paul gives to his son Timothy is that of the hardworking farmer (verse 6). The key idea in the model of the farmer is that of labor. The life of the farmer is characterized by hard work. The labor of the farmer is especially significant because it is always done with patience and is directed toward the harvest. The hard work of preparing the ground, planting the seed, cultivating, and watering the tender plants takes a lot of patience. There are no "instant results" in farming. And the one aim of all this patient labor is the harvest. That's what farming is all about. What lessons for the growing Christian! The Lord expects us to work hard in our service for Him even though there may not be "overnight success." The labor of the Christian in God's fields is sometimes very discouraging. Much patience is needed at times to sow the good seed of the Word of God and to cultivate the babes in Christ. But the harvest makes it all worth while. It is sheer joy for the hardworking Christian to see the Word he has planted take root in the heart and life of a person and finally result in a strong fruit-producing Christian. That is what it means for the Christian to "receive his share of the crops." And the reward does not end on this earth!

Paul gives other models to Timothy in the second chapter of this letter to Timothy. They are included in

God's Word as patterns for all faithful Christians to follow. We must confess that most of the time we are like peacetime soldiers, weekend athletes, and back-yard farmers. God is looking for soldiers who sacrifice, athletes who are disciplined, and farmers who labor.

14

Trust and Obey

Genesis 35:1-3   Then God said to Jacob,
"Arise, go up to Bethel, and live there; and
make an altar there to God, who appeared to
you when you fled from your brother Esau."
So Jacob said to his household and to all who
were with him, "Put away the foreign gods
which are among you, and purify yourselves,
and change your garments; and let us arise
and go up to Bethel; and I will make an altar
there to God who answered me in the day of
my distress, and has been with me wherever I
have gone."
For continuity read all of Genesis 25–35.

Trust and obey, for there's no other way
To be happy in Jesus, but to trust and obey.
   All to often we glibly sing the words of this familiar
Christian hymn without giving them much thought.
These important words convey exactly what the Bible
teaches. The secret of spiritual happiness and blessing
is simply trusting and obeying the Lord. Frequently

growing Christians think that the secret of being "happy in Jesus" is found in some other method, like "spiritual experiences." No! The divine method for happiness and blessing is full trust in God and complete obedience to His Word. Lack of faith and partial obedience not only result in unhappiness and loss of blessing; they bring serious consequences in the life of the believer.

The Bible contains many passages that teach the trust-and-obey-for-happiness principle (see Psalm 119, for instance). In addition, many character studies from the Scriptures illustrate this same truth. Jacob is one such example. Jacob was a believer who had to learn over and over again throughout his life that halfway trust and obedience do not bring happiness and blessing. Is it possible that some of us are experiencing depression because of lack of faith and partial obedience?

In Genesis 31 we meet Jacob returning to Bethel. He had just spent twenty tough years away from home waiting for his brother Esau's anger to cool. Jacob had become the target of Esau's wrath because he had cheated Esau out of certain family rights and blessings (Genesis 25–27). The fact that Jacob felt he had to cheat to get these blessings may be the first indication of lack of faith on Jacob's part. God had previously promised that Esau would serve Jacob (Genesis 25:23). Jacob did not have to jump the gun and manipulate the blessing from Esau. He could have "rested in faith" and waited on God to fulfill the promise in His own time and way. God has made many promises to us, too. He has promised to give us joy and contentment in Christ and He has promised to meet all our physical needs (see Matthew 6:33 and Philippians 4:19). We do not have to selfishly manipulate others or force God's hand. Waiting for God's timing is often difficult, but it is the best way in the long run.

Near the beginning of his long, sad journey away from home Jacob stopped to camp for the night (Genesis 28). At this point, of course, Jacob had no idea that he would be away from home for a long time or that he would never see his beloved mother, Rebekah, again. During the night God gave Jacob a dream, the well-known Jacob's ladder dream. In the dream, God declared His sovereign purposes for Jacob. God emphatically stated that He would be with Jacob, keep him, bless him, give him all the land that he was on, and eventually bring him back to his homeland (Genesis 28:13-15). What grace! God extends His grace to us in the same way. We fail Him so often with our halfhearted faith and obedience, but He is constantly faithful to His promises. "The LORD's lovingkindnesses never cease. . . . They are new every morning; Great is Thy faithfulness" (Lamentations 3:22-23). It is true that, like Jacob, we must reap the consequences of our lack of faith and token obedience, but God is gracious and will complete the good work which He has begun in us (Philippians 1:6). It is significant, in this connection, that Jacob is included in the "Hall of Faith" of Hebrews 11—but note that it is near the end of his days (Hebrews 11:21).

Jacob's response to God's declaration in the dream is again indicative of the little faith he had at this time. Although Jacob shows some faith by renaming the place Bethel (Genesis 28:19) which means "house of God," he hedges by vowing, *"If* God will be with me and keep me . . . and give me . . . and bring me back safely . . . *then* the Lord will be my God (verses 20-

21). Does this sound like any of our prayers of "faith"? What kind of trust and obedience is this! Perhaps it is better called selfish bargaining with God rather than faith in God. God had stated in no uncertain terms His promises to Jacob, and yet Jacob had the audacity to hold back with an "if" type of faith and obedience. But let's not mock Jacob's faith and obedience before we examine our own. Can we say without reservation that we simply trust and obey, or must we confess that we selfishly bargain with God? *"If* You help me pass this exam, God, I'll give more time to reading Your Word." *"If* You let me look good in this event, Lord, I'll witness for You." *"If* You help me out of this predicament, Father, I'll serve You more." This kind of trusting and obeying does not bring happiness and blessing. No wonder Jacob was not overjoyed with his experience in the presence of God. His reaction of fear and awe (verse 17) does not exactly convey happiness in Jesus. During the next twenty years in a land called Paddan-aram God taught Jacob that happiness does not come through a selfish kind of trusting and obeying.

In Genesis 31, the long years of discipline were over, and Jacob was ready to come home. He had taken some hard courses in the school of God, and the time had come for the Lord to send him back to Bethel, the place of the dream and the promises and the selfish vow (Genesis 31:3,13). Notice that in verse 13 the Lord honored even the little faith that Jacob exhibited in his selfish vow made years before. How gracious and condescending is our God! In obedience to the Lord's command, Jacob left Paddan-aram and traveled toward Bethel and Esau. Jacob had improved in trust and obedience! In Genesis 32, on the eve of the reconciliation with Esau, Jacob had a wrestling match with the angel of God. Here Jacob learned that he must be completely broken of self and rely fully on God for blessing. After such an experience with God we would be inclined to close the story of Jacob by writing: "Jacob was reconciled to his brother Esau and lived happily ever after and served the Lord wholeheartedly in godly trust and obedience." But the Bible doesn't give us any such fairy tale endings, because the Bible tells the life stories of real people. God's Word gives accurate descriptions of real people like you and me and Jacob. Jacob had certainly learned and matured and grown in his faith and obedience as a result of the twenty years of discipline which climaxed in the wrestling match (compare Jacob's prayers in Genesis 28:20 and Genesis 32:10). But all this was no guarantee that he would never fail in faith again, and that's exactly what we see in Genesis 33. We too may pass some long, difficult courses in God's school of discipline. We may even experience some traumatic wrestling matches with our God. He breaks us of self in order to bless us. As a result, we may make great strides forward in trust and obedience, but this does not mean that we are failsafe. Have you ever failed the Lord in the very area you thought you had just conquered and given to Him?

Let us see how Jacob failed to fully trust and obey the Lord in Genesis 33. After his reconciliation with Esau, who had traveled some distance to meet him, Jacob did not continue on his way back to Bethel in full obedience to the Lord's command. Instead he went in a different direction and settled in Succoth (Genesis 33:17). God had told Jacob to return home to his relatives and He would take care of him (Genesis 31:3). There was no need to continue to fear Esau. But Jacob once again turned aside from the path of trust and obedience. He apparently decided to stay away from Bethel indefinitely since he built a house and barns in Succoth (Genesis 33:17). As a result Jacob experienced more years of unhappiness and loss of blessing.

Living in Succoth brought many associated problems. Not too far away was the pagan city of Shechem. It was natural for Jacob to spend some time there with his family for business purposes. Perhaps he erected the altar nearby to justify his relationship with this pagan city (Genesis 33:18-20). But believers cannot play around with token trust and obedience and expect to go unscathed. Genesis 34 records the tragedy that took place in Jacob's family as a result of his not going back to Bethel. Jacob's daughter Dinah was abducted and raped, and his sons Levi and Simeon became liars and murderers. What a lesson for us! There is always a falling-out when faith and obedience are forgotten. And it affects others besides ourselves. God has given us many precepts and principles to guide our lives as growing Christians. His Word covers everything: control of thoughts, relation to parents, guidance in vocation, sex life, role of men and women, borrowing money, forgiving others. God does not expect us to question or change or compromise His commands; He expects us to simply trust Him and obey Him. That's the way to find spiritual blessing and happiness.

Jacob was finally ready to listen with both ears to God. In Genesis 35:1 God said to Jacob, "Arise, go up to Bethel, and live there; and make an altar there to God." Jacob got the message! The connections with paganism were severed, and in full trust and obedience Jacob came back to Bethel (verses 2-6). Here he built an altar (verse 7) and here God blessed him (verse 9).

If only Jacob had come back sooner! In ten or fifteen years will you look back and say the same thing about your life? "If only I had trusted and obeyed God more—right from the start!"

God continued to work in Jacob's life. God continues to work in our lives. There is no shortcut to graduation in the school of God. God wants to bless us and make us "happy in Jesus," but that cannot be unless we trust and obey.

15

Spiritual Blessings

Ephesians 1:3   Blessed be the God and
Father of our Lord Jesus Christ, who has
blessed us with every spiritual blessing in the
heavenly places in Christ.
Read Ephesians 1:3-14.

A beautiful way to start off the New Year is to
begin with a doxology—an expression of praise to God.
How much better this is than to begin the New Year
with a hangover! Only when people are in a proper
relationship to their Creator can they have a happy
year.

Ephesians 1:3-14 is a doxology. It is a response of
praise to God for the many spiritual blessings He has
given us. A number of spiritual blessings are listed in
this doxology, and it is important for the growing
Christian to understand them. When these blessings
are properly appreciated, they go a long way toward
making the New Year a happy one. Spiritual blessings
can only be seen by faith, because they are spiritual.

That is, they are not material blessings like a good job or a healthy body. They are blessings that cannot be physically seen or touched—they are spiritual. But being spiritual does not make them any less real. They are as real as any physical reality, but their existence and effect must be entered into by faith.

Verse 3 tells us that every spiritual blessing is ours in Christ. Because of our relationship and association with Christ, God has given us all the blessings that heaven ever knew. God does not withhold a single spiritual blessing from any Christian. Appreciating and appropriating these blessings, however, is a different matter. Let us not blame God for our lack of faith. These spiritual blessings are said to be in "heavenly places," which further emphasizes the fact that they are not earthly and physical. The idea in the phrase "heavenly places" is not a location in space somewhere (note that the word "places" is in italics in your Bible) but rather the realm of spiritual experience and activity into which we are brought because of our identification with the risen Christ; thus, we do not enjoy our spiritual blessings by some kind of mystical experience, but rather by simply believing that what the Bible says about our blessed position in Christ is true.

The first spiritual blessing that is mentioned in this doxology is our *election*. Verse 4 tells us that we were chosen in Christ before the foundation of the world. God "rubber-stamped" us for heaven away back in eternity past! We must admit that this is a mindblower of a concept, but any attempt to water it down (for example: God chose only those whom He foresaw would choose Him) infringes on the sovereignty of God. To limit God's omniscience (all knowing and knowing all) some time in the past is to limit God.

The Bible also teaches that every human being is responsible to choose God and that God has given every person enough data in order to make that choice (see Romans 1:18-20). No one has an excuse for not choosing God and no one is "rubber-stamped" for hell. It is beyond our finite minds to fully grasp how these two seemingly contradictory truths harmonize. However, they are not logically contradictory. If the Bible said that God both chose and did not choose or that man is both responsible and not responsible, then we would have a contradiction in logic. But no, the Bible teaches that God chooses the saved while the lost do not choose God. No person in heaven will be able to brag, "I'm here because *I* chose God." And no person in hell will have as an excuse, "I'm here because God didn't choose *me.*" Yes, this is difficult to understand, but then we have finite minds which cannot completely fathom all truths. The important point here in Ephesians 3 is that God wants me to appreciate the fact that He handpicked me (with all my problems and sin which He forever knew) to become holy and blameless before Him forever. And there was no good thing or merit within me (see Romans 3:10-18) to cause Him to do it. This is a spiritual blessing indeed!

A second spiritual blessing is mentioned in Ephesians 1:5. We are *predestined to sonship* in the family of God. The word "predestined" not only emphasizes the sovereignty of God once again but also indicates that the subjects are foreordained for a purpose—in this case, adoption as sons. Adoption in New Testament days was an official act by which a boy was placed in the position of an adult son. No longer was he treated as a mere child or servant. He now had all the privileges, responsibilities, and dignity associated with sonship. When we become Christians we are not only born into the family of God; we are also placed in a position of full privilege in the family. The manifestation of our sonship awaits the resurrection, but it is a fact now. Think of this tremendous spiritual blessing. Out of the kindness of His heart, God picked us individually as sons—not slaves, but sons! (See also Romans 8:15-17 and Galatians 4:4-7.)

Redemption and *forgiveness* are two more spiritual blessings that come to our attention in Ephesians 1:7. Before salvation, we were in bondage to sin and slaves of Satan. This was actually true whether we realized it or not! But the Son of God came down to the slave market and redeemed us. The ransom price was high: He bought us back at the cost of His own life. Now Satan has no claim on us. The price has been paid and we are free to follow our Savior. The Lord Jesus is not a slave-driver—He is the Lord of love. He has not only redeemed us but He has completely forgiven us for running away. What a Redeemer! No wonder Scripture goes on to say that all this was according to the riches of His grace which He lavished on us.

Another spiritual blessing is that we now have the *capacity to understand God's eternal purpose* for the universe (verses 9-10). What is this purpose? It is to put all things (people, places, powers, planets, professors) under the visible authority of Christ at His second coming. The plan was not fully revealed to the Old Testament saints. That is why it is referred to as the "mystery of His will"—not mysterious, but previously secret. Now this eternal purpose of God has been made known. Christians have been given insight and discernment into God's program for the future. This is a spiritual blessing. Think of the unbelievers all around us who are struggling for security and peace of mind in a world they see as chaotic and futile. Little do they know that present powers and politics are programmed for complete change. What a blessing it is for the believer to know that his future does not depend on the selfish plans of a power-hungry politician or the itchy fingers of a future push-button war machine.

The fact that we are going to *share in God's glorious program* for the future is another spiritual blessing (verses 11-12). When our Lord comes back to claim this world for His own, we will be with Him and will be part of His visible and eternal kingdom. What an inheritance! And we will actually participate in the everlasting glory of our Lord Jesus Christ. Can it really all be true? Look at us now: a group of Bible-believing and Jesus-preaching evangelicals. As far as the world is concerned we are duped and to be pitied with our "wishful thinking." By faith we continue to hold onto our spiritual blessing because the Word of God says it is true. "Our Lord Jesus Christ . . . has given us new birth into a living hope through the resurrection of Jesus Christ from the dead, and into an inheritance that can never perish, spoil or fade—kept in heaven for you" (1 Peter 1:3-4, NIV).

In Ephesians 1:13-14 the *Holy Spirit* is mentioned as another spiritual blessing. Two facts are stated here about the work of the Holy Spirit. We are sealed with the Spirit and given the Spirit as a pledge of our inheritance. A first century seal on a letter or container indicated ownership and security. In the same way, God has sealed every Christian with the Holy Spirit. He owns us because of the finished transaction at the cross. We are stamped secure in Christ. And God won't take His seal back or permit it to be broken. What a blessing to know that our salvation is sure and secure! As a pledge, the Holy Spirit is like a down payment or an engagement ring. He is a guarantee of what's to come for us in the future. We look forward to the redemption of our bodies as part of our inheritance. As God's own possession, not only is the salvation of our souls secure (the seal) but the complete redemption of our bodies is guaranteed (the pledge). Some day we are going to have new bodies which will be immune to suffering and sickness and sin—forever. (See also Romans 8:23; 1 Corinthians 15:51-54; 2 Corinthians 5:1-8; Philippians 3:21; 1 John 3:2).

This magnificent doxology in Ephesians comes to a close with verse 14. Perhaps you noticed that the doxology is in three stanzas: verses 3-6, verses 7-12, and verses 13-14. Each stanza concludes with a note of praise to the glory of God. Although the main emphasis of the doxology is on the spiritual blessings of the Christian, it is interesting to note that in each stanza our attention is drawn to a different Person of the Trinity: God the Father in the first stanza, God the Son in the second stanza, and God the Holy Spirit in the third stanza. Such is the beauty of the structure of Scripture. Our spiritual blessings are from the Triune God. By faith let us claim and enjoy every spiritual blessing that God has given us and enjoy a happy New Year.

16

Living Sacrifice

Romans 12:1   I urge you therefore,
brethren, by the mercies of God, to present
your bodies a living and holy sacrifice,
acceptable to God, which is your spiritual
[rational or intelligent] service of worship.
Read Exodus 3:15-18; 8:25-28; 10:8-11; 10:24-26.

We sing and talk a lot about Christian service.
At many retreats and rededications we have presented
ourselves as "living sacrifices" to the Lord. But very
often the living sacrifices crawl off the altar before the
offerings can take place. God strongly urges us in Romans 12:1 to present our bodies to Him as a means
of rational or intelligent service. There can be no real
service for Christ until we are willing to present *ourselves* as a sacrifice. *We* must be holy. *We* must be
acceptable. Otherwise all our so-called Christian service is just a lot of singing and talking!

Satan knows Romans 12:1 as well as any Christian.

He knows that if he can keep a Christian life from being holy and acceptable then there is not much value to the sacrifice. Satan knows that the advance of the kingdom of God in this world is not by song and talk but by "living and holy sacrifice."

In the great story of the Exodus we learn that God wanted His people to leave Egypt and travel three days into the wilderness to serve Him by offering sacrifices (Exodus 3:15-18). But the enemy, Pharoah, did everything in his power to keep the people of God in Egypt—far from the appointed place of sacrifice and service. God has given us this account in His Word to show us how the archenemy of the Christian operates to keep us from presenting ourselves as living sacrifices. Pharoah tried four different tactics to keep the people from leaving Egypt and sacrificing to the Lord their God. Satan uses the same four tactics today to persuade Christians to compromise in their offer of themselves as living sacrifices to the Lord.

In Exodus 8:25 Pharoah says, "Go, sacrifice to your God within the land." The devil approves of sacrifice as long as it is "within the land [of Egypt]." Egypt represents the world. This is where the enemy is king. Satan is king even in the "religious world." He encourages "religion." He applauds the works and actions of individuals seeking self-glory under the guise of religious service. Satan knows that every man has a vacuum in his soul which can only be filled with the living God. If Satan can fill a soul's void with the religious activity of the world, he is still king of that life. True Christianity is not religion but a living relationship with God through Jesus Christ. And the Lord's command is that we leave the land and go "three days' journey" to sacrifice (verse 27). The three days certainly suggests the journey of our Lord through death and resurrection. That's what "living sacrifice" is all about. Have we travelled with the Lord through His death and resurrection? Are we committed to Him to the point where we have died to self and have risen with Him? (See Colossians 3:1-3.) Or are we content to pretend and play at Christian service "in the land of Egypt"?

In Exodus 8:28 the second tactic of Pharoah is employed. "I will let you go, that you may sacrifice to the LORD your God in the wilderness; only you shall not go very far away." If Satan cannot keep us in the land he will try to keep us close to it. Here all the deceptions of the enemy are readily available to suck us back in and destroy our testimony. A borderland Christian is not a "living and holy sacrifice"! A student who fellowships and prays with Christians one night but parties with the world the next is not an "acceptable sacrifice." Even the ungodly know that this is not rational or intelligent Christian service. They smile at the hypocrite who says Jesus is number one and then does not do what Jesus commands. Jesus calls us to go *"three days' journey* into the wilderness" to sacrifice. Yes, it is easier to live near the pleasures and treasures of Egypt than to live as a sacrifice in the wilderness. (See Hebrews 11:24-27.)

The third tactic which Pharoah used in his attempt to get the people of God to compromise is found in Exodus 10:11. "Go now, the men among you." That is, the men can go and sacrifice but leave the family behind. Pharoah knew that if he held onto the wife and kids, dad wouldn't be able to serve the Lord very efficiently for long. If Satan cannot get us personally to stay in his territory, his strategy is to get us tied in by our closest relationships. How successful the devil has been with this tactic! Many men and women have failed in this area. They purpose in their hearts to present their bodies a living sacrifice to God and then end up presenting them to someone else. The lesson is obvious. 2 Corinthians 6:14 says, "Do not be bound together with unbelievers." Presenting your body to anyone other than God's choice is unholy and unacceptable. The Lord already has a Christian partner picked out for you. A living sacrifice is willing to wait.

Exodus 10:24 gives us Pharoah's final attempt to keep God's people from total commitment. "Go, serve the LORD; only let your flocks and your herds be detained." How subtle! Leave your livelihood in Egypt. Satan knows that if our careers and other interests and "things" are left in his realm he still has some control. We may think that we are strong and separated Christians, but if one of our deepest motives is to get ahead in this world on its terms, then our flocks and herds are still in Egypt. There is only one answer: "not an hoof will be left behind" (verse 26). Leaving Egypt completely, in total commitment as a living sacrifice, raises some basic questions that we must ask ourselves. Am I planning my career to get *me* ahead in this life or have I presented it as part of my "living and holy sacrifice" to the Lord? Are my possessions used to serve the Lord or are they "hoofs" still holding me to Egypt? Until the "flocks and herds" leave Egypt there can be no sacrifice (verse 26). Until then, Christian service is only song and talk!

Worship, relationships, career, interests—all must make the three days' journey. Everything about us must bear the stamp of our new resurrected life in

Christ. This kind of Christian service is holy and acceptable to God. This is living sacrifice.

17

Five Fantastic Facts

Ephesians 1:23   The church . . . is His
body, the fulness of Him who fills all in all.
Ephesians 2:6   God . . . raised us up with
Him, and seated us with Him in heavenly
places, in Christ Jesus.
Ephesians 2:22   You also are being built
together into a dwelling of God in the Spirit.
Ephesians 3:10   The manifold wisdom of
God [is now being] made known through the
church to the rulers and authorities in the
heavenly places.
Ephesians 5:32   This mystery is great; but
I am speaking with reference to Christ and
the church.

Some Christians have the idea that when you
are born again you get a ticket to heaven and "fire
insurance" and that's about it. To be sure, that is more
than enough to be an unbelievable bargain but there
is even more to our salvation—much more! The book
of Ephesians is loaded with facts about the whole pack-

age that God gave to us when we became Christians. These facts are fantastic in their magnitude. If it wasn't for Scripture they would be practically unbelievable because they so boggle the mind. Let us look at five of these fantastic facts and as a result praise God for His infinite love to us.

Ephesians 2:6 tells us that we are seated with Christ in heavenly places in Christ Jesus. What does that mean? Let's break this fact down by phrases. "Heavenly places" is not some place in the universe but rather the heavenly state or new realm of spiritual experience and activity into which we are brought upon conversion. "In Christ Jesus" has to do with our status before God now that we have entered "heavenly places." Because of our identification and association with the risen Christ by faith, God now sees us in Christ. This is our status or standing or legal position before God. We no longer stand as guilty and condemned sinners before the holy and righteous Judge of this universe. The Judge now sees us as righteous because we are "in Christ Jesus." This is not our own righteousness (obviously!), but rather Christ's righteousness which is imputed to all who are "in Christ Jesus."

"Seated with Him" further defines our status or position in Christ. We can see from Ephesians 1:20-22 that the main idea of Christ being seated (enthroned) is His exaltation and supremacy and authority. The fact that we are "seated with Him" means that positionally we are now associated with Christ in His exaltation. Now this is a fantastic fact! What a position we have in Christ and what far-reaching implications. Can there be any question as to our secure and permanent salvation if we are already enthroned with Christ in glory as far as God is concerned? No wonder we are

urged in Ephesians 3:12 to have confidence and bold-
ness to enter into God's presence, for that is our present position in Christ. (See also Hebrews 10:19.) Let
us walk in the light of this fantastic fact.

Another fantastic fact is given to us in Ephesians
1:23. Here we are told that the church, which is the
body of Christ, is the fulness of Him who fills everything in every way. Before we explain this fact, let it
be noted that the four remaining fantastic facts all deal
with Christians collectively. Our exalted position in
Christ (2:6) seems to be an *individual* matter, but these
other facts have to do with the church as a whole.
Whenever the church is mentioned in Ephesians, it is
the universal church that is in view and not the local
church. All true Christians everywhere constitute the
universal church not some particular organization or
denomination.

Ephesians 1:23 states that the church (universal) is
the body of Christ and is the fulness of Christ. As a
physical body is the full complement of its head, so
the church is the full complement and expression of
Christ. The Lord Jesus Christ is head over the church,
not only because He is sovereign over all (1:22) but
also because we are His body. As the body of Christ,
we are the means by which our Head expresses Himself
in this world. What a fantastic fact—but what a responsibility! We are inseparably linked to the One who
"fills all in all." Christ is not only the source and sus-
tainer of His body but of the universe as well. (See
also Ephesians 4:10 and Colossians 1:17.) As individual
members of the body of Christ, let us relate to one
another and to this needy world in ways that fully reflect the thoughts and interests of our Head.

A third fantastic fact is found in Ephesians 2:20-22.

Here the church is likened to a building under construction. The foundation has already been laid. Now individual Christians are being "fitted together" like building blocks according to God's blueprint. The blueprint is of a "holy temple in the Lord." The temple is not complete yet but the building is "growing" toward that goal. It is significant that the word "growing" is more of an agricultural term than an architectural term. The church is a living building, composed of "living stones" (1 Peter 2:5). Thus, membership in a local church is not what makes a person part of the building. Life in Christ is essential for living stones. Organic union is necessary. The church is an organism and not an organization.

The most fantastic aspect of this unfinished organic building is that God dwells in it now. The church with all her faults and failings is even now the dwelling place of God on earth in the Person of the Holy Spirit. We are not yet the glorious temple that God intends us to be forever, but already we are the home of the Spirit of God. In 1 Corinthians 6:19 we see that our individual bodies are the temples of the Holy Spirit, but here in Ephesians we further see that together we are the temple of the Holy Spirit. (See also 1 Corinthians 3:16.) This tremendous spiritual truth should be worked out practically in our Christian living. We should not think, for example, of any man-made building with stained glass windows as the residence of God. God is in the midst of His people wherever they meet, be it a sanctuary or a storefront. Furthermore, as the home of the Holy Spirit, we should give Him the right to move around as He desires. Let us not box Him in by limiting His freedom of expression to only a few official stones in His building. 1 Peter 4:10 says that

He has given special gifts to every living stone. (See also Ephesians 4:16 and the word "every.") Finally, since we are being built into a "holy temple" of the Holy Spirit, let us be a holy people.

In Ephesians 3:10 we have a fourth fantastic fact. The church is said to be God's object lesson to unseen powers. What is all this about? The Scriptures indicate that angels have access to the spiritual realm called "heavenly places" which was described above. Ephesians 6:12 indicates that even certain of the fallen angels have access to this realm at the present time. Now at first this seems hard to grasp, but when you think of the spiritual struggles and battles we have (consider your prayer life, for example), we begin to understand a little of what the Scripture is talking about. The fantastic fact is that God is now making His wisdom known to all these powers through the church. Angels are not omniscient. They eagerly observe and learn the wonders of God's infinite wisdom (1 Peter 1:12). Angels saw the power of God displayed at creation (Job 38:7). They have seen many aspects of God's wisdom throughout history as God has dealt with man. But the full wisdom of God is now seen through the church. We are the highest channel of God's wisdom, higher than any other created thing in this vast universe. How do angels learn about the love of God, for example? They cannot experience it as we can, for they are not a redeemed people. Angels observe and learn the love of God through His people. What a lesson in love they learned when they saw the eternal Son of God leave heaven and become man for the express purpose of giving His life to save sinners like you and me. No wonder the angels are joyful when a sinner repents and is added to the church (Luke 15:10). And no wonder the angels are very interested in how we respond to the authority structures that God has set up in creation and in the church. (See 1 Corinthians 11:10.) The church was ordained from eternity (Ephesians 3:11) to be God's masterpiece for the universe. How dare we distort God's master plan?

A final fantastic fact comes to our attention from Ephesians 5:32. This verse is the climax of a heavy exhortation to husbands and wives regarding their responsibilities to one another. We are informed that the relationship between husbands and wives portrays the relationship between Christ and the church. The fact that this relationship is a "mystery" does not mean that it is something mysterious. Whenever the New Testament uses the term "mystery" it is referring to truth which was hidden in Old Testament times but is now revealed. (See Ephesians 3:4-5 for the scriptural definition of "mystery.") The fact that the church is the bride of Christ is a fantastic thought. We not only have the life of Christ as His body but we have the love of Christ as His bride. As the beloved bride of Christ we have His care, protection, concern, intimate fellowship, and unending love. What more could we ask for? And what a model on which to pattern our own marriages!

We've looked at just five fantastic facts from Ephesians. There are others. Read the entire book and see how they build on one another. Growing Christians receive a spurt in growth when they digest the fantastic facts of Ephesians.

18

Divorce Is Not an Option

Malachi 2:16   "For I hate divorce," says the
LORD.

"If things don't work out we can always get a divorce." All too often these days we find that this is the unspoken attitude of persons contemplating marriage. The old-fashioned ideas of "for better or worse, for richer or poorer, in sickness and in health, till death do us part" don't carry much weight in our society any more. My life and my happiness and my sexual fulfillment are most important. And besides, if both partners more or less agree to a divorce, why not? Why should two potentially dynamic individuals stifle themselves by trying to grind it out over the years, only to remain static and unfulfilled and miserable? Divorce is so much easier and better and more beautiful! This present day concept of marriage may sound quite reasonable, but it is definitely contrary to the Word of God. Growing Christians must be extremely careful that they do not get brainwashed by current social thought. Our culture is constantly exerting enormous pressure on us. If we are not careful, we are unknowingly moved to conform to our culture's way of thinking. Any Christian who considers marriage in the near future (yes, that may be you) needs to be reminded that according to the standards of Scripture, divorce is not an option when the honeymoon is over.

Divorce is not a biblical option because God says, "I hate divorce." It is significant that this verse comes to us from Malachi, which was written at the close of the Old Testament period (fifth century B.C.). Even though divorce had become very commonplace in Israel by this time, God had in no way lowered His standards with the passing of time. God had given His concept of what marriage was to be in the beginning when He brought the first man and the first woman together. God had declared that "a man shall leave his father and mother, and shall cleave to his wife; and they shall become one flesh" (Genesis 2:24). Man was not to separate what God had joined together. That was our Lord's comment concerning the divine institution of marriage (see Matthew 19:5-6). We dare not make divorce an option, unless we have a low view of God and His Word.

Divorce had raised its ugly head within the circles of God's people as early as Moses' day. Most likely the people of Israel had picked up the idea of "divorce on demand" during their long stay in Egypt where divorce was prevalent. It is true that the law of Moses did permit or tolerate divorce (Deuteronomy 24:1-4), but this allowance was certainly not divinely sanctioned or approved. In fact, when our Lord was questioned about this section of the law (see Matthew 19:7-9), He made

it very clear that divorce was never a divinely sanctioned option: "from the beginning it has not been this
way." Notice that the Lòrd even changed the words of
the Pharisees' question in order to drive home the
point that divorce was of man and not of God. They
asked, "Why did Moses *command* . . . ?" Jesus answered, "Moses *permitted.* . . ." The permission was
not because God approved divorce but because man's
heart was hard (stubborn and perverse). Divorce has
never been a God-approved option, either before the
law, under the law, or under grace. The sins that God
in His grace forgives in no way become any less sin
than they were "from the beginning."

Our Lord went on to declare that divorce was tan-
tamount to adultery (Matthew 19:9). The strictness of
this "narrow" view is confirmed by the disciples' reaction (verse 10). In light of such Scripture, can any
Christian reasonably take a more lenient position than
the Son of God concerning marriage and divorce? If
Jesus is Lord, then divorce cannot be an option, regardless of changes today in concept, culture, or
church.

The Lord Jesus gave only one exception to the no-
divorce rule. If one partner in the marriage is unfaithful to the other, then divorce is permitted. This permission was not given to encourage divorce but rather
to rigidly forbid it for any other cause. The reason that
divorce is permitted for adultery is that this sin is of
such a nature that the very concept of marriage is
broken. Marriage is consummated when the man and
woman become "one flesh" in physical union (Genesis
2:24). When physical union takes place outside of marriage the one-flesh reality still holds as specifically
stated in 1 Corinthians 6:16. Thus in the case of adul-

tery, the original divine yoke is broken and divorce is permitted as a legal recognition of the break which has already taken place in the sight of God. The unfaithful partner will one day have to answer to the Lord Himself for daring to sever a bond which "God has joined together" (Matthew 19:6).

Why does God hate divorce? Because the severing of the divine union distorts the important truth that God wants to convey through the marriage bond. God ordained marriage not only for the purposes of propagation and enjoyment but also to model the relationship between Himself and His people. The constant and permanent love and care and forgiveness that God extends to us is to be replicated in marriage. This concept is not the wishful thinking of some romanticist removed from the real world but rather the direct teaching of Scripture. In Ephesians 5:22-33, husbands and wives are commanded to reflect the love relationship between Christ and His church (verses 22-29). The truth of our union forever with Christ is to be portrayed in the bond of marriage (verses 30-31). What a revelation! No wonder the Scripture calls the one-flesh reality a great mystery (verse 32).

Divorce shatters the picture. The wonder and beauty and depth of the love relationship between Christ and His church cannot be communicated through a broken marriage. When problems develop in a marriage (and no marriage is without its tensions), every effort should be made to restore the perfect model. Even these efforts can be part of the picture. Christ continues to love and forgive and restore His church with all its imperfections. Working marriages can reflect this dynamic relationship, but divorce can never mirror the on-going relationship between us and the Lord. For this reason, even in cases of unfaithfulness, the ideal solution would be forgiveness rather than divorce. (Read the book of Hosea in this connection.) Yes, divorce is permitted for the faithful partner, but it is not demanded. Restoration and reconciliation are far more in line with how God deals with His people. We can praise God that He doesn't opt for divorce every time we are unfaithful to Him!

"But is it worth it all?" some Christians ask. "Why shouldn't I get a divorce anyway? I admit that it's wrong and that God's beautiful plan will be destroyed but divorce is still better than years of an unhappy marriage. Besides, I'll just be one of many forgiven divorcees in heaven. And don't tell me you haven't made a lot of mistakes yourself—you just happened to be lucky in your marriage, etc." Such reasoning is common among Christians these days, and it does contain a certain logic. But it is shallow thinking. Is it possible to be truly happy in this life knowing that you've severed a divine bond and that you're out of the will of God? What about the future? Our position in eternity should certainly carry more weight in our thinking than our pleasure now. Will it not be worth it all to some day look confidently into the eyes of our Savior and hear Him say, "Well done, good and faithful servant" (Matthew 25:23)? How much better than to "shrink away from Him in shame at His coming" (1 John 2:28).

Some of you are not married yet and may be asking at this point: why all the concern? Let's just say that it's preventive counseling rather than crisis counseling. If, through this writing, a few growing Christians are brought to see the importance and seriousness, as well as the wonder, of marriage, then it will have served its purpose. Since God hates divorce, then we can be sure that He is equally concerned about helping us make the right choice in marriage. Don't rush into marriage. Wait on God for His choice and remember Proverbs 3:5-6. The Lord knows our needs and our desires. "Delight yourself in the Lord, and He will give you the desires of your heart" (Psalm 37:4).

Some of you who are reading this are married and may even now be struggling to keep your marriage together. Remember that God is still a God of miracles. As He can heal a diseased body, so He can heal a troubled marriage. He can even supernaturally give you a new love which was never there before. Working at marriage is not always easy, especially when divorce is so convenient and no longer a stigma within our culture. God's Word teaches that divorce is not an option. For many Christians this a difficult doctrine to swallow. Sound doctrine is not always easy to handle. Paul challenged Timothy to endure sound doctrine as well as hardship (2 Timothy 4:3-5). Timothy was told that the time would come when many would not endure sound doctrine. They would rather listen to teachers who were preaching what they wanted to hear. How true today! Many Christians refuse to endure the doctrine of marriage as taught by our Lord Himself. Growing Christians are challenged to submit to the Word of God and recognize that divorce is not a biblical option.

19

Controlled by Context

Philippians 4:13   I can do all things
through [Christ], who strengthens me.

It is well-known that if you quote people out of
context you can have them say just about anything you
want. We all know that politicians are expert at this
craft—especially around election time! Unfortunately,
that's exactly what some people do with the Bible. It's
amazing what the Bible can be made to say if it is
quoted out of context. In fact, it's often said that a
biblical text out of context becomes a pretext. That is,
it is used for the purpose of presenting ideas which
are more in line with the mind of the speaker than
with the mind of God.

Now most Christians do not deliberately pull Scripture out of context. We all have our pet peeves and
axes to grind, but let's hope that we don't willfully
twist and distort Scripture to serve our own purposes.
However, many Christians unwittingly take Bible

verses out of context by ignoring the context. In fact, it is sad to say that most Christians habitually run the risk of pulling Scripture out of context because they do not give enough attention to the surrounding context.

Let us take Philippians 4:13 as an example of what it means to be controlled by context. What does the Bible mean when it says, "I can do all things through Christ, who strengthens me"? Does it mean that I can lift five hundred pounds if I have enough faith? Does it mean I can jump off a ten-story building and not break a bone because I have supernatural strength? Does it mean I can walk on water as Christ did on the Sea of Galilee? Certainly no Christian in his right mind takes Philippians 4:13 that far out of context. But what about the following cases?

Consider those Christian students who take on too great a work load—academics, athletics, action groups, and other wholesome activities. They go without proper rest and constantly push themselves to take on more load. Is it right for these students to claim Philippians 4:13 for "success" in all of these areas? Does the context of this verse allow such a claim? Should such students feel they have failed in faith or that the strength of Christ has failed them if they end up on the verge of burn-out? Has the promise of Philippians 4:13 proved false—or has the verse been taken out of context?

Consider further the Christian man or woman who launches out into a new career or even a new ministry for the Lord without first doing some serious preparation and wise planning. Does Philippians 4:13 predict prosperity as long as the strength of Christ is claimed in faith? Suppose the new career doesn't work out or the ministry folds. Is it right for the Christian man or woman to be frustrated and disappointed with the Lord because Philippians 4:13 doesn't work? Is the strength of Christ really good for "all things" or has Philippians 4:13 been twisted out of context?

Contributing even further to the confusion concerning the proper interpretation of Philippians 4:13 are those Christians who use the verse to explain why they are so successful in various endeavors. Take the Christian businessman, for example, who quotes Philippians 4:13 in his talk at a testimonial dinner to account for his financial success. This sounds pretty good at first, but where does that leave all the poor struggling Christian businessmen and women in the audience who are not doing so well financially? Isn't the strength of Christ good for them too? Has Philippians 4:13 been taken out of context? Or what about the record-setting Christian athlete who humbly quotes Philippians 4:13 to explain the triumph? It all sounds so great and it certainly comes from an attitude of praise, but when this verse is used as an explanation for athletic accomplishments it raises a serious question. Again we must ask about the Christian athletes who are not so talented and did not win any medals. They also trained and tried their hardest but they either lost or never even qualified. Where was the strength of Christ for them? Certainly many of them had as much faith in the promise of Philippians 4:13 as the winning Christian athlete. Was this verse pulled out of context again?

The problem in all the examples above is that the context of Philippians 4:13 was ignored. The use of this verse by all those well-meaning Christians was not

controlled by the context, and thus the verse was made
to say things that were never intended by the Holy
Spirit. Context is so important for our appreciation
and application of Scripture. Studying the context is
not only helpful but mandatory for the proper interpretation of any passage of Scripture. Checking out the
context safeguards us from interpretations that God
never had in mind when He inspired the text. A good
understanding of the context acts as a control over our
ideas of what a particular verse means. Knowing the
context eliminates the need for guesswork and "inspired imagination"! There is less "I think it means
. . ." and "I feel it means . . ." kind of interpretation
when the context of a passage of Scripture is
comprehended.

What exactly do we mean by "context"? Context is
more than just the surrounding verses of any text of
Scripture. Context means the surrounding paragraphs
and chapters and ultimately the entire book of the Bible in which the text is located. The more we come
to know the historical background, original occasion,
and the intended purpose of that book, the theme, the
structure, and the argument of that book, the more
we will be helped and controlled in our interpretation
of any text in that book of the Bible. By the way, this
is why one of the best ways of studying Scripture is
the book-by-book method. God did not compose the
Bible by putting together isolated verses here and
there, but rather He gave His Word by books. Why not
study it the way God gave it? This is not to say that
topical studies or meditations on favorite passages or
even just-open-and-read-anywhere approaches to the
Bible cannot be profitable. But studying the Bible by

books has the added advantage of coming to know what is so vital for proper interpretation: the overall context of any verse in that book.

The basic and obvious reason why understanding context is so important is that God did not write a single verse of Scripture without a context. There is always a historical context and a literary context to any verse in the Bible. Therefore the question of "What does this verse mean to us today?" should always be preceded by "What did this verse mean when it was written?" What was the historical situation? Who was writing and to whom was he writing? When and where and why was this Scripture written? What type of literature was used? Was it prophecy, parable, poem, letter, historical narrative, or some other form of literature? Knowing the answers to these questions is all part of knowing the context of the verse, and this knowledge enables us to properly proceed from "What did it mean then?" to "What does it mean now?" Once we've done this homework, our applications for today will be more sound and less speculative because they are based squarely on God's original intention of the text.

Now let us look briefly at the context of Philippians 4:13 and see how even an abbreviated contextual awareness can help us with the interpretation of this verse. The apostle Paul was a prisoner in Rome when he wrote this letter to the Philippians. (See Acts 28.) The church at Philippi was founded about ten years previously, on Paul's second missionary journey. (See Acts 16.) A Christian brother named Epaphroditus (Philippians 2:25; 4:18) had come from Philippi to Rome with a financial gift to help meet Paul's needs. One of the purposes for the letter to the Philippians was to thank the believers there for their gift and to explain Paul's situation in Rome. Now notice the verses immediately surrounding Philippians 4:13. Paul was very thankful for the gift and also for the fact that the Philippians were concerned about him (verses 10,14-19). The apostle also stressed (verses 11-12) that regardless of his circumstances he was content because he had learned to depend on the Lord to meet his needs. It is in this context that we have the confident statement of verse 13. In times of need and hardship Paul was not worried because he had come to know from experience that he could depend completely on Christ for strength. And we can too! *That* is the wonderful promise of Philippians 4:13 for us today—in context!

Guided by context control, we see that we shouldn't claim Philippians 4:13 for financial success or good grades or gold medals, but we certainly can claim it for strength in time of need. Remember also, from the overall context, that the needs that Paul faced were all because of his service for Christ, not hardships resulting from selfish ambition or irresponsibility or negligence. This should further control our interpretation and application of this promise for today. Are you facing any needs or difficulties or hard times right now because of your decision to stand for Christ? You can claim with all confidence, "I can do all things through Christ, who strengthens me."

20

Defeat at Ai

Joshua 7:5   And the men of Ai struck down about thirty-six of their men, and pursued them from the gate as far as Shebarim, and struck them down on the descent, so that the hearts of the people melted and became as water.
Read all of Joshua 7–8.

"**D**efeat at Ai" is not a misprint! Ai was an ancient city located near Jericho. It was not as large and strong a city as Jericho, but it became very significant because it was there that Israel suffered a major defeat. Now that may not seem very important to us today, but we must remember that every defeat of God's people recorded in the Old Testament contains lessons for God's people today. (See Romans 15:4 and 1 Corinthians 10:11.)

Is there such a thing as defeat in the life of a Christian? Yes, but it does not have to happen! The Bible tells us that we are involved in spiritual warfare and that Satan is doing everything he can to defeat us. (See Ephesians 6:12 and 1 Peter 5:8.) The Scriptures also tell us that Satan is a very clever and subtle enemy and tries every trick in the book to cut us down (Ephesians 6:11 and 2 Corinthians 2:11; 11:14). Doubts about our faith, discouragement in our ministry, depression concerning our circumstances, and despondency over our future are just a few of the "flaming missiles of the evil one" (Ephesians 6:16). Our enemy has a whole arsenal of weapons for spiritual attack against us. If he cannot tempt us to quit the battlefield (Satan is quite successful with this tactic!), his aim is to slash away at us with his weapons until we despair and fall defeated on the field of spiritual battle. Unfortunately, this takes place to one degree or another in the lives of many growing Christians. But again it must be stressed that defeat is not necessary. In fact, defeat should not be part of normal Christian experience. Battles, yes; defeat, no! God has given us all the armor (Ephesians 6:13-18) and tactical strategy necessary to be continually successful and victorious in spiritual warfare. However, we must confess that much of the time we are careless and disobedient soldiers.

Let's look at a few of the reasons for Israel's defeat at Ai and see how these apply to our spiritual battles today. The first reason is given to us in the first verse of chapter 7. Israel disobeyed the Lord. How? God had explicitly told His people (Joshua 6:17-19) that when they conquered Jericho they were not to take any of the spoils of Jericho for themselves. But we read (7:1,21) that a man named Achan stole some of the silver and gold which was to go into the treasury of the Lord and hid it underneath his tent. Achan probably reasoned that his little cut of the booty wouldn't be missed. Certainly such a small amount would not affect the treasury of the Lord or the welfare of the people. But God saw it differently! Achan's sin of disobedience was the primary reason for the defeat of all Israel at Ai. God emphasizes this fact in His Word by stating it twice, both before (7:1) and after the defeat (7:11). Think of it—one man's sin affected the whole camp of Israel! Not only did Achan's sin result in defeat at Ai, but God declared (7:12) that the whole nation could not move forward and that the whole nation would not have the Lord's help and presence unless the sin was judged. Remember, this is all because of one man's secret sin which started with a mere look. Look at verse 21 again and notice the snowballing effect. "I saw . . . I coveted . . . I took. . . ." Little did Achan realize that his personal and private sin would affect all Israel. What about our secret sins?

The name Achan means "troubler." Achan became a troubler for all Israel. Are you an Achan? Is the spiritual growth and progress of the group with whom you fellowship stifled because of your sins? Is the presence of the Lord and help from the Lord limited, or hindered, within the church or Bible study you attend because of your personal and private sins? These are heavy and maybe disturbing concepts, but they are scriptural. God sees the fellowship as a whole. We cannot sin in a vacuum. We are not islands unto ourselves. Like Achan, we don't begin to see the far-reaching effects and consequences of our selfish sins until it is too late.

Achan's sin was not that he robbed Jericho or even his own people—He robbed God. Do we rob God? We can rob God by wasting time, because it is His time. The same could be said in reference to the abilities that God has given us, as well as our material possessions. All of our time, talent, and treasures belong to the Lord. The idea that only a certain percentage is the Lord's and the rest is ours to use or abuse in any way we choose is foreign to the Scriptures. We are robbing God when we fritter away our time watching "nothing" on TV. We are guilty of robbing the treasury of the Lord whenever we use our natural talents or acquired skills (as well as our money) to do things which are not pleasing to the Lord. Sometimes the Lord's treasury is robbed in the name of hobbies, or extracurricular activities, or rest and relaxation, when such good things are carried too far. God would teach us from Joshua 7 that such robbery is not only sinful, but it leads to spiritual defeat in our own lives and detrimental effects on the spiritual growth of our brothers and sisters in the Lord. Are we guilty of this sin? Are we defeated and causing defeat in the lives of fellow believers, because we have robbed God of what rightfully belongs to Him?

Another reason for Israel's defeat at Ai was overconfidence. We see in verse 3 that Israel was so self-confident that they figured only two or three thousand men were needed to conquer Ai. How wrong they were! We see from Joshua 8:25 that their estimate of the enemy's strength was much too low. Overconfidence will do this every time. Fear will make the enemy appear larger, but overconfidence will make the enemy appear smaller. Both extremes are wrong for the Christian warrior. We are not to cringe in fear before Satan, and we are not to think we can fight him in our own strength. Our confidence must be in the Lord. "Be strong in the Lord, and in the strength of His might" (Ephesians 6:10).

We growing Christians are particularly vulnerable to the problem of overconfidence right after a spiritual victory. That's the way it was at Ai. Israel had just won a major victory at Jericho. They were still at a spiritual high point. How could little Ai possibly pose a threat when the mighty walls of Jericho had just been toppled? And yet defeat was just around the corner. Let us be careful that a "little" problem, like impatience or silly talk or coarse joking (Ephesians 5:4), doesn't trip us up while we're celebrating our victories over the big Jerichos like materialism or bitterness or lust.

Associated with Israel's overconfidence was another reason for defeat at Ai. There was no communication with the Lord. We do not read of Joshua and the elders of Israel coming to the Lord in prayer until after the defeat (Joshua 7:6-9). No wonder the Lord told Joshua to get up off his knees (7:10). There was no need to ask God why Israel was defeated (7:7). God had clearly promised continuous victory to Israel if they would obey Him. (See Joshua 1:7-8.) Now was the time to judge the sin. Continual communication with the Lord is essential for growing Christians. Many casualties of spiritual warfare would be eliminated if we would fall to our knees before the battle, not after we've experienced defeat.

Israel's sin had to be dealt with decisively. The fact that Achan's family was stoned and burned along with Achan (Joshua 7:24-25) may seem like a rather harsh judgment, but it probably is a good indication that the family was also guilty. After all, it would have been rather difficult to bury treasure inside the home tent

(7:21) without the family being aware of it. In any case, the lesson for us is pointed. We must deal ruthlessly with that which brings defeat in our lives before it brings further defeat. Is materialism bringing defeat in your Christian life? Then give away your material! Do you have a problem with unhealthy literature or art? Then don't buy or read or browse or even glance at unhealthy paperbacks or magazines. This is what our Lord meant in Matthew 18:8-9.

As Israel passed in review before the Lord (Joshua 7:13-18), so we should examine ourselves in His presence and let His Word point out those things in our lives that are causing defeat. (See Psalm 139:23-24; Hebrews 4:12). Then there must be confession of sin (Joshua 7:20). But confession is not enough. The root cause of the defeat must be removed before full fellowship with the Lord can be restored (7:26). In Joshua 8 we see that when we return to the Lord, even our defeats at Ai can be changed into victories. Such is the grace of God toward growing Christians.

21

New Age Manipulation

2 Corinthians 2:11   We are not ignorant of [Satan's] schemes.
2 Corinthians 4:4, NIV   The god of this age has blinded the minds of the unbelievers, so that they cannot see the light of the gospel of the glory of Christ, who is the image of God.
2 Corinthians 11:14   Satan disguises himself as an angel of light.

What is the New Age movement? Some Christians have never even heard this term. Other Christians have dismissed the New Age movement as just another branch of humanism which has been greatly overplayed and unduly attacked by a small group of fanatical Christians. Most Christians have heard New Age terminology bandied about but are still fuzzy in their comprehension of what the movement is all about. To begin with, there really is a New Age movement, but much of it is hidden because many of the groups do not label themselves "New Age." More importantly, the movement is not neutral but rather ominous, and therefore growing Christians need to become aware of the underlying thought patterns and goals of this movement. Concisely defined, the New Age movement is a worldwide network of loosely interconnected organizations and groupings which ultimately are all committed, more or less, to a "new world order" in which exists worldwide political and religious unity and harmony. Almost all of these groups are heavily influenced by Eastern religious thought and advocate meditation, yoga, and other self-help methods for realizing and developing the individual's inner wisdom and spiritual potential. Spiritual/mystical experiences which enable the individual to tap into or attain unity with a "higher" or "cosmic" consciousness of "force" are also advocated by many of these groups. The mental transformation that these experiences bring about opens the way for people to learn "advanced" habits and attitudes. Most New Agers maintain that this is the basic means by which the goal of global unity will be attained. If this description of some basic New Age ideas sounds totally foreign to you, read on. Many Christians are largely unaware of the subtle ways the New Agers are infiltrating our society with their ideology.

As growing Christians, we need to be discerning and on the alert about the New Age movement. Behind all the hype of the New Age scenario is the hiss of the age-old serpent. On the surface, the push for worldwide peace and unity appears very noble and admirable, but below the surface this movement is actually being masterminded by Satan himself. The New Age movement is, in reality, a worldwide manipulation of human souls. People are being manipulated to pave and prepare the way for a notorious world leader of the end times—the Antichrist. Under the guise of a better world for all mankind, Satan is maneuvering for a massive takeover through people who have become his unsuspecting pawns.

The first clue that the New Age movement cannot be from God is that the core groups involved patently and plainly deny that Jesus is God. Although many New Agers use a lot of biblical language, quote the words of Jesus and refer to Him as a god, the bottom line is a denial of Jesus as the only Son of God—the God of the Bible. Even a cursory investigation of the New Age movement should convince any growing Christian that this movement is not neutral and harmless but actually satanic and dangerous. The fact that New Agers are kind and loving and their ideology has an appearance of innocent humanitarianism should not be surprising. The Bible teaches that this is one of the ways the enemy of souls operates. Three Scriptures in 2 Corinthians describe Satan's devious tactics.

According to 2 Corinthians 2:11, we are not in the dark as to what Satan is up to in this world. Why? Because the Bible clearly informs us of the devil's perennial strategy. Ever since he fell into sin, Satan's aim has been to take away from the glory of God by thwarting God's purposes in this world. His schemes are designed to keep non-Christians from coming to Christ and to keep Christians from being effective for Christ. One of Satan's most successful methods in accomplishing his goals is the gaining control of our culture, or the overall thought patterns and concepts of our society. This strategy is effective because the culture in which we live influences our mind-set and way of thinking so very greatly—whether we like it or not!

Satan doesn't care whether the culture is characterized by capitalism or communism, humanism or hedonism, asceticism or atheism, as long as the cause of Christ is countered. One of the scheming tactics that Satan employs to gain control of any culture or subculture is to counterfeit Christianity by starting false movements. Satan-inspired movements always have a measure of truth and goodness about them because imitation and deception have always been one of the devil's chief ways of ensnaring souls. Religious movements that are not Christ-centered are counterfeit movements. They look good on the outside but are inspired by Satan at the core. Communism, for example, looks appealing with its apparent emphasis on people and equality, but its basic atheistic philosophy proves it is one of Satan's counterfeit movements. The New Age movement is one more of the enemy's counterfeit schemes. It appears plausible to the unsuspecting and uninformed, but behind the mask of all the sweet-talk about peace and unity and beautiful experiences lies the scheming mind of Satan. As Christians, we long for worldwide peace and unity, but we know it can only come about through the return of Christ. No New Age counterfeit messiah can bring true and lasting peace. Let us not be deceived or manipulated by a scheme that ultimately denies the Lord Jesus Christ—the one and only Prince of Peace.

2 Corinthians 4:4 informs us that unbelievers are blinded by Satan. In what area has the god of this world blinded the people of this world? He has blinded them to the "gospel of the glory of Christ who is the image of God." Satan doesn't mind if Christ is recognized as a great human leader and teacher. These facts don't save anyone! Satan's aim is to keep the light

of Christ's glorious deity and this gift of salvation from people at all costs. The devil has designed all kinds of mind-blinders for people to put on so that the divine light is blacked out. The New Age movement is one of them. All the promises of the age of Aquarius are part of this satanic cover-up. Satan's tempting promise in the garden of Eden that "you shall be as God" is still blinding people today. The great emphasis on human potential and "the force within" as well as the "god is all/all is god" presupposition in New Age thinking continues this lie and blinds unbelievers to their lost condition. The use of the beautiful and peaceful rainbow as a symbol also has the effect of keeping people off their guard. Only in the light of the good news of the glory of Christ are the subtleties of the New Age movement exposed. That light is shining all around, and even though Satan tries everything he can to block that light from unbelievers, he can never put out that eternal light.

In 2 Corinthians 11:4 we learn that Satan is able to hide his true identity, using a most disarming costume. Who would ever think that an angel of light would like to see people separated from God forever? But that's exactly where the New Age movement for global peace and unity will lead its followers. To be sure, there are peaceful experiences along the way. The mystical experiences attained through altered states of consciousness are not just imagination. Such experiences are real, but they are manipulations by the angel of light. Satan knows that such experiences of "cosmic oneness" help to blur the distinction between the Creator and His creation. Some New Agers even claim to have met an angel of light and other "ascended masters" in their mystical trips. These spirit beings all talk of peace and love and unity, but always apart from the supremacy and deity of the Lord Jesus Christ. On the basis of the Scripture before us, we know that these so-called ascended masters and spirit guides are, in reality, demonic spirits masquerading as angels of light.

As growing Christians, we do not deny the possibility of God-given spiritual experiences, but they will always be Christ-centered and biblically based. The temptation to seek mystical experiences through transcendental meditation, yoga, self-hypnosis, and other altered conscious state techniques is not of God. It is rather an open door to the world of Eastern religion and the occult. In fact, growing Christians need to be very careful and leery of relaxation and visualization techniques which can very easily be used as first steps to the dangerous altered consciousness states. Stress management seminars, if not biblically based, can be used to teach these types of techniques. Many of the widely advertised self-help tapes, videos, and courses which claim to teach people how to overcome bad habits and develop greater personal potential are promoting these New Age techniques. And we should not be surprised if the angel of light is doing his best to introduce some of these New Age methods into the church in Christianized garb. Beware of Christian education seminars advocating non-biblical types of meditation and visualization techniques. Be wary of church seminars giving assertiveness training or personal potential development courses. These courses could be used by Satan, the angel of light, to turn our focus from God's power at work in us to our own human potential. What subtle manipulation!

There is a new age coming, but it will not come

about through the New Age movement! God will bring about global unity with the return of Christ (Revelation 22:1-3). In that great day the throne of the Lamb will be established, the nations will be healed, and the curse of sin will be lifted. Is there any better description of true global peace and prosperity?

22

Investment in Wind

Hosea 8:7 They sow the wind, and they reap the whirlwind.
Hosea 12:1 Ephraim feeds on wind, and pursues the east wind.

Whoever heard of an investment in wind? How ridiculous! We ought to have our heads examined if we fall for the sales pitch of a person selling wind. But wait a minute. Maybe you are investing in wind! You may be dipping your hand into the overflowing pot of this life's activities and grabbing nothing but a fistful of wind. But I'm a Christian, you say. Yes, but Christians can invest in wind, too. We're not talking here about our eternal salvation, of course. That's settled and secure once we acknowledge the Lord Jesus as our personal Savior. But it does matter how we growing Christians build on the foundation of Jesus Christ. (See 1 Corinthians 3:10-15.) Our dividends in heaven are determined by what we invest in on earth. We can invest in eternal sureties, or we can invest in wind.

Some Christians invest heavily in cubic yards of wind. Are you buying wind?

Israel invested in wind. The story of God's people in the Old Testament is a sad commentary on a people who had so much going for them, but then destroyed it all because they turned away from God to pagan idols. God certainly sent them plenty of securities advisors but they still invested in nothing of substance. Is it possible that some of us are as blind as Israel— surrounded by God's advice and warning but still investing in nothing but wind?

In the prophecy of Hosea we have a very dramatic portrayal of Israel's bad investment. It is seen as an analogy to Hosea's marriage. (See Hosea 1–3.) Hosea provided love, care, security, and protection for his wife, Gomer, but she turned away and was unfaithful to him. Chapter 3 indicates that she actually sank to the level of a prostitute slave. Yet Hosea still loved her! He bought her back and brought her home. What a picture of God's love and faithfulness to His unfaithful people. We can praise the Lord that this picture of God is just as true today as it was in Old Testament times.

In chapters 4–14 of Hosea, the unfaithfulness of Israel to the Lord is described in more detail. The figure of wind is used, along with other picturesque speech, to vividly convey Israel's sad condition. Three statements are made about God's people in reference to the wind, and all three have an important practical application for Christians today. God said that Israel was sowing the wind (Hosea 8:7), feeding on wind (12:1), and pursuing the east wind (12:1). These descriptions are all different aspects of investing in wind.

In the figure of "sowing the wind and reaping the whirlwind" we have in view the law of the harvest and the law of multiplication. According to the law of the harvest you reap what you sow. If you sow wheat, you reap wheat; if you sow weeds, you reap weeds; if you sow wind, you reap wind. The law of the harvest operates in the spiritual and moral realms as well as the physical. "Do not be deceived, God is not mocked; for whatever a man sows, this he will also reap" (Galatians 6:7). The people of Israel had invested their time and resources and energies in that which would bring no eternal benefits. The folly and futility of their idolatrous way of life is succinctly captured in the figure of "sowing wind." Are you sowing wind? Write out a list of all the activities you are involved in at present, and then check off the ones which will still matter one hundred years from now. Quite a bit of wind left, isn't there? We should guard against sowing too much time, energy, and money on clothes and recreation and parties and other means of self-indulgence. We will reap nothing in terms of our eternal well-being from these seeds. No wonder growing Christians are exhorted to "guard yourselves from idols" (1 John 5:21). Idols are not just the wood and stone types that Israel turned to, but anything that steals our hearts and minds away from total commitment to the Lord. Irresistible idols are but seeds of wind; they yield nothing but a wind harvest.

The law of multiplication means that you get back more than you put in. Sow a few wheat seeds and you reap a field of wheat; sow a few dandelion seeds and you reap a golden lawn; sow the wind and you reap the whirlwind. "Whirlwind" implies not only more wind but devastating and destructive wind. Like the law of the harvest, the law of multiplication also holds in the moral and spiritual realms. If we invest our lives in the nothingness of what this world has to offer, we not only reap a harvest of nothing but we destroy our lives as well. Many Christians have lives that are disordered, chaotic, and shattered because of their investment in the wind of this world. The law of multiplication demands that the cyclone come! It is only a matter of time before a believer's life is totally destroyed if he persists in sowing wind. "The one who sows to please his sinful nature, from that nature will reap destruction" (Galatians 6:8, NIV).

In Hosea 12:1 Israel is pictured as feeding on wind. Ephraim, by the way, is just another name for northern Israel. Hosea's message was for all Israel, but was addressed primarily to the northern ten tribes. What does it mean to feed on wind? Did you ever try a wind sandwich? Wind does not satisfy your hunger or nourish your body. There is no sustenance and there are no nutrients in wind. The people of Israel were feeding their souls with all the things of the good life and feeding their spirits with the words of the false prophets. Hosea's day was much like our own day. There was plenty of material prosperity on the outside, but the heart of the nation was morally and spirtually bankrupt. Instead of turning back to the Lord to satisfy their spiritual hunger, Israel continued to feed on wind. They stuffed themselves with the attractions and allurements of the surrounding pagan nations and filled themselves with the all-too-appealing words of the false prophets. But they ended up empty and starved.

Today it is possible for a believer to follow the same pattern as Israel. Never before has there been such an attractive array of "wind food" around for the Christian. And it's not just the junk food available through certain movies and TV programs. There are all kinds of wind salesmen around with appealing programs to ensnare you. Getting heavily involved in secular clubs and associations rather than Christian fellowship or becoming experts in a particular hobby at the expense of our spiritual health are examples of wind programs. Even our studies and career, which can consume enormous amounts of our time and energy, may become a feeding on wind if God is left out of the picture. We may feel fulfilled and satisfied now, but what about later? We must have a steady diet of the solid food of the Word of God now if we are going to avoid the stunted growth, starvation, and emptiness that are associated with feeding on wind. Remember that "man shall not live on bread alone, but on every word that proceeds out of the mouth of God" (Matthew 4:4). Let us be careful of what we munch on—we don't want to lose our appetites for the Word of God.

We also read in Hosea 12:1 that Israel pursued the east wind. The east wind is the terrible and dreaded sirocco which blows from the desert east of Palestine. It comes with scorching and devastating heat. Instead of trying to escape or seek protection, Israel is pictured as actually chasing this east wind. How was Israel pursuing the east wind? The rest of verse 1 gives us an example. Israel was double-dealing with the great foreign powers of that day. She made a peace treaty with Assyria, but at the same time she exported oil to Egypt, Assyria's arch rival. How's that for foreign policy? Playing both ends against the middle for security was as foolish as chasing the sirocco for tranquility. Instead of turning to the Lord for peace and security, Israel turned to foreign powers which would ultimately destroy her. It wasn't long before Assyria swept in like the east wind and thoroughly wiped out the northern kingdom of Israel.

How foolish of Israel, we say. But are we not just as foolish when we look away from God to "foreign powers" for our peace and security? Why do we hoard? Doesn't the investment policy of Matthew 6:33 carry enough security for us? Why do we become anxious and worry so much? Isn't the promise of Philippians 4:6 good enough for us? Why do we spend so much time in pursuit of the good life? Doesn't our Lord's statement in John 10:10 carry enough weight for us? Maybe a lot of us need to rethink our investment policy and make sure we are not pursuing the east wind. Chasing the east wind will not only fail to bring peace and security to us; it will eventually lead to our being utterly destroyed—nothing of eternal value to our name.

When Solomon, the wisest man who ever lived, reflected on everything under the sun, he came to the conclusion that, apart from God, "all is vanity and striving after wind" (Ecclesiastes 1:14). The nation of Israel did not follow King Solomon's advice. Let us growing Christians be wise before the Lord and not invest in wind.

23

Carmels and Caves

James 5:17   Elijah was a man with a
nature like ours, and he prayed earnestly that
it might not rain; and it did not rain on the
earth for three years and six months.
Also read 1 Kings 17–19.

Elijah! What's the first mental picture that
popped into your mind when you read the name, Elijah? Well, if you remember anything from the Old Testament account of Elijah, you probably visualized a
fearless prophet dressed in rough wilderness garb, calling down fire from heaven. That's Elijah, all right, on
Mount Carmel. There on that mountain Elijah cou-
rageously spoke out against the religious idolatry of
his day. He called fire down from heaven and proved
to the people of Israel that the pagan gods called Baals
were nothing but helpless idols. But Mount Carmel
was not the only place visited by the prophet Elijah.
We also read of him in a cave at Mount Horeb. Chances

are that this picture of Elijah did not come to your mind. Elijah's cave experience is not nearly as well-known as the Carmel event. The "cave crisis" was not exactly a high point in Elijah's ministry. In fact, the cave at Mount Horeb was a spiritual low in the life of this great prophet of God. However, God used this valley experience as a further turning point in Elijah's ministry. Our text says that Elijah was "a man with a nature like ours." All growing Christians experience spiritual highs and lows. There are the Carmels and there are the caves. Let's trace the path of Elijah from the triumph of Carmel to the trauma of the cave and learn a few of the lessons that God has for us in 1 Kings 17–19.

Elijah came on the scene at a time when Israel had not only turned away from the Lord but had also begun to follow the pagan religions of the surrounding nations. Long gone were the good old days of the united kingdom under David and Solomon. The kingdom was now split into the southern kingdom of Judah and the northern kingdom of Israel. Jeroboam I, the very first king of northern Israel, put his kingdom on the downhill road of idolatry by setting up two golden calf idols for the people to worship. All ties with the true worship of the Lord at the temple in Jerusalem (capital of the southern kingdom) were severed. No wonder the biblical record of the kings of Israel repeats over and over that "Jeroboam made Israel sin." Elijah was raised up as a prophet of God to the northern kingdom about forty years after Jeroboam, during the reign of wicked King Ahab. Ahab continued to lead Israel into idolatry. He built a temple for the degrading Baal worship in Samaria, his capital city (1 Kings 16:28-34). He married the idolatrous foreigner, Jezebel, who encouraged the prophets of Baal and the Asherah, a pagan female deity, to prosper in Israel and actually live at government expense (18:19). The evil Jezebel systematically killed off many prophets of the Lord (18:4,13). Thus Ahab "did more to provoke the Lord God of Israel than all the kings of Israel that were before him" (16:33).

Suddenly Elijah stepped into this picture of religious apostasy. Such idolatry called for confrontation and judgment. However, before the confrontation at Carmel could take place, the nation had to be forced to realize that God's blessing had been withdrawn from the land. The people had to realize that the gods which they were now worshiping were not helping them one bit. For three and one-half years there would be no rain—not even dew (1 Kings 17:1). Israel knew that rain was a sign of God's blessing, according to His covenant promises (Deuteronomy 28:12). They also knew that a prolonged drought meant that God was punishing them (verse 24). And the rain that God would not provide, the pagan gods could not provide. For three and one-half years Israel was conditioned by God for the showdown at Carmel. We logically ask at this point, how stupid could the people be to go on following the helpless and lifeless Baals? Could we not just as logically ask the same question about our own nation today? Our country appears bent on self-destruction as it increasingly forsakes the God of the Bible and His blessings to serve other gods. Perhaps the "droughts" of recent days (oil, for example) are conditions that God has permitted to bring the nation to its knees, or to a Mount Carmel type of judgment.

While the nation of Israel was "reaping what it had sown," Elijah was being prepared for Mount Carmel. After telling Ahab that the nation's water shortage problem was going to last for years (not weeks or months), Elijah disappeared from public view. For the next couple of years God taught His prophet about His miraculous ways of provision and protection. Remember, it was a time of drought and famine, and Jezebel was out to kill every prophet of God, especially Elijah (1 Kings 18:10). But God has His ways of protecting and providing for His servants. Have you come to know God as the One who can provide for you and protect you in any and all situations? What about when you don't get your paycheck? What about when someone is determined to discredit you? Like Elijah, every growing Christian must learn to depend on God alone, to gain confidence in Him as an all-caring and all-capable God. Only then are we ready for the Mount Carmels.

Mount Carmel was close to enemy territory. Nearby Phoenicia was the former home of Queen Jezebel and the source of many of the prophets of Baal. It seems that Elijah purposely chose this location so that there would be no possible question raised later on about "home field advantage." Now Elijah, having learned confidence in the Lord, boldly challenged the prophets of Baal to get their god to answer by fire (1 Kings 18:24). He also challenged the crowd from Israel who had gathered for the excitement. "How long will you hesitate between two opinions? If the LORD is God, follow Him, but if Baal, follow him" (18:21). Is it possible that the same question is being asked of you? Are you hesitating between a life choice of serving gods like materialism or the good life and the choice of going all out for the Lord who created you and gave His life for you?

Baal, of course, was no match for the Lord! How could the demonic powers behind the Baals even begin to compare with the omnipotence of God? Elijah mocked the pagan prophets as they carried on their "Come on Baal, light my fire" ritual! We may laugh at their pathetic ravings now, but these pagan prophets were as serious then as many of our friends are today—selling their souls to the gods of this world in exhausting but futile activity. When it was quite obvious that Baal had failed, Elijah calmly and confidently repaired the altar of the Lord and then inundated the altar, wood, sacrifice, and surroundings with water. He didn't want the unbelievers to back out with an excuse like, "It must have been some kind of trick!" It was no trick when the fire of the Lord fell. It consumed everything, even the water. The only reason the fire did not consume the false prophets was that they were left for the people to take care of—a responsibility they should have taken care of long before. (See Deuteronomy 13.)

The climax of the triumph at Carmel was the coming of the rains. Elijah was so filled with the joy of the Lord and so thrilled with the way everything had worked out that he outran Ahab's chariot to Jezreel, a town about thirty miles away! Talk about spiritual highs! But it was a short-lived mountaintop experience. No sooner had they reached Jezreel than Elijah was ready to throw in the towel. Why? Because things did not go as he had expected when they got to Jezreel and to Jezebel. Elijah thought that on the basis of what Ahab had seen at Carmel, the king would turn back to the Lord and send wicked Queen Jezebel packing. But instead, Ahab merely reported the day's happenings to Jezebel, who in turn threatened to kill Elijah within twenty-four hours. Elijah turned and ran for his life. He didn't stop running until he had put about three hundred miles and a lot of wilderness between himself and Jezebel. He told the Lord along the way that he wanted to die because he was a failure (1 Kings 19:4). We would never say anything like that, would we? And then at Mount Horeb Elijah crawled inside a cave to continue his self-pity. What a comedown: the mighty Elijah pouting in a cave. We shouldn't be that surprised. "Elijah was a man with a nature like ours." Don't we drop rapidly from mountaintop to valley? Yes, and like Elijah, we are always more vulnerable right after a spiritual triumph. And like Elijah, we are particularly susceptible to discouragement and disillusionment when we are occupied with ourselves and our ministry rather than with the Lord Himself. Notice Elijah's emphasis on himself and his ministry when he answered the Lord's probing question, "What are you doing here, Elijah?" What is our response when God asks us the same question?

The grace of God is certainly emphasized throughout God's dealings with Elijah, even at the cave. Not only did God care for His fatigued servant on the way to the cave, but He graciously taught His shortsighted servant in the cave. Elijah learned that God speaks not only by hurricanes and earthquakes and fire from heaven, but also by the gentle voice (1 Kings 19:11-14). Elijah learned that he was not the only believer still faithful (19:18). Elijah also learned that God recommissions His repentant servants (19:15-17). Every growing Christian needs to learn these same lessons. They go a long way toward overcoming the "cave mentality" as well as inhibiting the "Carmel-to-cave" cycle.

24

Rewards for Giving

2 Corinthians 9:8, NIV   And God is able to
make all grace abound to you, so that in all
things at all times, having all that you need,
you will abound in every good work.
Read all of 2 Corinthians 8 and 9.

Christian giving is supposed to be from the
heart. The motive of love, and not the desire for rewards, should be the driving force behind Christian
giving. The idea of getting something in return or the
attitude of "What's in it for me?" must be foreign to
true Christian giving. This guideline for giving is quite
familiar to every growing Christian, even though we
don't always practice what we preach. But now that
we've stated this well-known point about Christian giving, we should also note that the Bible does talk about
rewards for Christian giving. The Scriptures very definitely teach that giving is a good action. Just because
Christians are not to give for ulterior motives does not
mean that there are no rewards available! While the

basic motive for giving is not to be rewards, there are rewards nonetheless for faithful Christian giving.

In 2 Corinthians 9, at least seven rewards for giving are mentioned. In this chapter (as well as in chapter 8 which stresses principles of giving) the Corinthian church was being called upon to give to the poor church of Jerusalem. (See 1 Corinthians 16:1-4.) Although the context here concerns the giving of money, the application can be extended to all areas of Christian giving: our time and our talent, as well as our treasure.

One of the rewards of giving is seen in 2 Corinthians 6: *You will receive unlimited blessings.* There is no ceiling or cut-off to these returns. Even the most lucrative schemes or sweepstakes in this world have limits to their purses, but not so with Christian giving. The amount of blessing that we reap is limited only by our manner of sowing (Luke 6:38). The proper sowing attitude is not just "sow big," but sow "on the basis of blessings." This is a more precise translation of the word that is rendered "bountifully" in some translations. To sow "on the basis of blessings" means that we should be involved in doing things which bring help and happiness to other people. Giving help to the student who has unfortunately missed some classes or planning a happy surprise for some forgotten senior citizen is sowing "on the basis of blessings." Let us not give sparingly (verse 6) or hold back in a stingy way, but rather let us give purposefully (verse 7) and willingly (verse 7) and cheerfully (verse 7) and on the basis of blessings. Then we ourselves will reap on the basis of blessings. We will receive unlimited help and happiness in rewards. These blessings may be material and tangible, but they may also be intangible. The reward of unlimited blessings is not proven by statistics but by your own experience. Try giving and see for yourself!

The next two rewards of giving are found in verse 8: *Your own needs will be met* and *you will always have resources for giving.* God is willing and able to supply us with everything·necessary to meet our personal needs as well as the needs of our ministry of giving. Notice that the Scripture does not say that the Lord will give us all that we want. God knows us better than we know ourselves, and He promises to meet our true needs, not our many selfish wants. The promise of verse 8 definitely extends to our needs in Christian service. We can never use the excuse, "I don't have anything left to give!" God promises to supply all the needs of every ministry He's given us. Note the heavy emphasis is this verse on the "alls" of God's promise: All grace in all things at all times with all needs for all good works! Verses 10 and 11 also emphasize this promise of a constant supply for giving. *You will be supplied* with plenty of seed for sowing (verse 10) and *you will be enriched* in everything for all liberality (verse 11). In Christian giving, the well never runs dry!

The word "grace" (verse 8) in this context certainly indicates that God is thinking of more than just material needs. What do you need—more strength to get through this semester? More love for your roommate? More understanding of your parents? More courage to stand for Christ? More help or helpers for the ministry that God has given you? More tolerance for Christians who do not want to help in your ministry? More tenderness with people who rub you the wrong way? More ideas for your fellowship group? Well, it's all there! Everything you need as an individual child of God and anything you need for the areas of responsibility which God has given you are readily available. But remember that we are talking about rewards for Christian giving, not gifts for miserly, hoarding Christians who are unwilling to share in the areas of time, talent, and treasure.

A fourth reward of giving is stated in verse 9: *Your record of giving will endure forever.* Now that's something to think about! Long after the records of famous heroes and stars of this world are forgotten, the record of simple Christians who gave of themselves will be remembered forever. Verse 9 is a quotation from Psalm 112:9. This psalm refers to the actions and rewards of the godly person. "His righteousness" does not refer to salvation but rather to the righteous deeds of the godly One. These righteous deeds will remain forever because they will be published in eternity. Your Christian giving of time and effort and unsung "putting out" may not be recognized or appreciated now, but it will be for all eternity. So keep your sights set on retirement in heaven, not Florida. You can take it with you when it comes to your record of Christian giving. In fact, all believers will take their record of Christian giving with them into eternity. It is a sobering thought that for some Christians this will not be much of a reward.

Another reward of giving emerges from verse 10: *Your returns will be according to the natural law of multiplication.* The law of multiplication goes beyond the principle of "you reap what you sow." God has designed the laws of nature so that you reap more than you sow. This most incredible principle is just as true and miraculous in the spiritual realm as in the natural. What a fantastic reward for those Christians who think they have only a drop in the bucket to give! The law of multiplication says that one drop can be multiplied into bucketfuls! Give a drop of your limited ability to the evangelistic project on your campus or in your church and a whole community of people can be blessed. Give a drop of your busy schedule to share the gospel with your neighbor and a whole life can be turned around for God. Give a drop of your hard-earned cash to the printing and distribution of just one Bible in a foreign country and the living Word of God can be read and obeyed for years by many believers. Yes, our limited giving can continue to ripple out in ever-widening circles, even after we've left this earth. The Lord of multiplication can do unbelievable things with our few little seeds, but the law of multiplication cannot begin to operate without any of our seed.

A sixth and further reward of giving comes to us from verses 11-13: *You are given credit for contributing to the glory of God.* We see in these verses that the results of the Corinthians giving to the church of Jerusalem went far beyond the mere supplying of the needs of the saints. Thanksgivings actually ascended to God in heaven. And these thanksgivings brought glory to God. Here's where Christian giving differs significantly from the giving of this world's charitable organizations. While we can be thankful for, and contribute to, some of these good organizations that assist worthy causes, we must recognize that they do not give specifically in the name of Christ as in true Christian giving. Giving directly in the name of Christ not only meets needs but carries with it the reward of contributing to the glory of God. Normally we don't think of this reward when we make an encouraging phone call to a hurting brother, or we write a letter to a sister with a low self-image, or we give a few dollars to help send a child to a Christian camp. But as thanksgivings ascend to God from the recipients of our giving, we are given credit for contributing to God's glory. And the glory of God is really what life is all about when all is said and done. Investment in the supreme theme and grand plan and purpose for this universe is a super reward!

A seventh and final reward of giving is mentioned in verse 14: *You will be prayed for by others.* How many people are praying for you right now? Some Christians only get prayed for when they're sick or elderly or backslidden. As we begin to give of ourselves we find that a solid foundation of prayer support begins to materialize beneath us. How important it is for believers to have a broad backing in prayer, especially when we realize that life involves warfare against spiritual forces (Ephesians 6:12). Every little bit of Christian giving not only meets the needs of others but builds prayer protection and support for the giver in return.

Verse 15 is certainly a fitting conclusion to this section of Scripture on Christian giving. All rewards of giving are only possible because God gave Himself for us. "Thanks be to God for His indescribable gift!"

25

Broken Cisterns

Jeremiah 2:13 For My people have committed two evils: They have forsaken Me, The fountain of living waters, To hew for themselves cisterns, Broken cisterns, That can hold no water.

In Bible lands, a cistern was an artificial reservoir dug in the earth or hewn in the rock for the collection and storage of water. Cisterns were very important in Palestine because of the long dry season and the relatively few natural springs. But a broken cistern was practically worthless. Cracked rock or crumbling masonry could not hold water. Collecting and storing water in a broken cistern was about as smart as carrying a sieve for a canteen!

Jeremiah used the illustration of broken cisterns to point up the extreme foolishness of God's people, Israel. It should be emphasized that this illustration was not just thought up by Jeremiah as a sermon filler. More precisely, the Lord Himself originated and used this illustration in the prophetic message that He communicated to His people through His prophet Jeremiah. (See verses 1-2 and 4-5.) The message was spoken as a rebuke to the people who were no longer totally committed to their God. Certainly the broken cistern sermon has an application for God's people today.

To appreciate the full impact of the broken cistern message, let us look a little more closely at the historical context of Jeremiah 2:13. Jeremiah lived and preached in a day when the nation of Judah had turned away from the living God to do their own thing. No longer were they devoted to the Lord or depending on Him to meet their spiritual needs. They had turned away from the fountain of living waters and were looking everywhere else for something to quench their spiritual thirst. They dug for themselves cisterns of idolatry and immorality in the hopes that the fleshly pleasures of these sins would satisfy their needs. (Read all of Jeremiah 2.) But Israel found that the cisterns of their own making were broken cisterns and could hold no water, not even a little bit.

Notice that the text seems to indicate that the cisterns did not become broken after some time of holding water. No, they were broken from the time they were formed. They never held any water. This is always true of cisterns of our own making. Self-made attempts and schemes designed to find spiritual fulfillment apart from God will inevitably result in failure. They are doomed from the start. Only God Himself can quench our spiritual thirst. (See Isaiah 55:1-2, John 4:10-14, John 6:35, and John 7:37-38.)

How foolish of Judah to turn away from the Lord who had done so much for them. This made them guilty of two evils. Trying to construct an artificial reservoir for collecting spiritual water was bad enough, but committing the double evil of deliberately turning away from the life-giving spring was tragic. No one in his right mind would do such a foolish thing. Imagine yourself as a very thirsty person in a parched land, turning away from a bubbling spring of cool water to hack out a cistern for yourself under the hot sun, in hopes of collecting some rain water. If there was no natural spring around, this would be about the best thing you could do: dig a cistern and try to gather some water. If there was a natural spring nearby and you didn't know about it, you would be in a very pathetic situation, but at least you could be pitied for your diligent efforts in trying to collect some water. But if you did know that there was a good spring of running water readily available and you deliberately turned your back on this life-giving source to construct a cistern, you would be extremely stupid and foolish. No sympathy or pity could be generated for you when your quarrying efforts resulted in broken cisterns. This is precisely the illustration that God painted in words to show His people how utterly foolish and guilty they were when they turned away from Him. The surrounding heathen nations at least could be pitied. They ignorantly followed lifeless gods who could not meet their spiritual thirst. Furthermore, these pagan nations, unlike Judah, were loyal to their gods (Jeremiah 2:10-11). Israel knowingly forsook their source of living water for self-made broken cisterns. No wonder the heavens are called upon to be appalled and shudder at such foolishness and stupidity and evil (verse 12).

Is it possible that some of God's people today are

guilty of the same two evils that Israel committed in Jeremiah's day? Is it possible that we've become so accustomed to the living water that we've wandered away from the fountain to see if there's some water available elsewhere? Have we foolishly gotten involved in constructing cisterns of our own? What about our priorities in what we read, for example? Some Christians spend enormous amounts of time in newspapers and magazines and other secular literature but they spend little time (if any) in the Scripture. Why? Perhaps this is a form of cistern making. The point is not that it's wrong to read newspapers and magazines, but it is rather a question of our desires and what excites us. If we're leaving the living Word to spend all kinds of time in secular literature in order to satisfy ourselves in some way, we may be guilty of the same sins as the nation of Judah. What about our vocational pursuits? If Christians look for complete fulfillment in their vocations (Sunday-morning-only Christians), this could be a form of cistern making. The same thing goes for entertainment and recreation. All of these endeavors, of course, are not wrong in themselves and are even good and helpful for a balanced life. But when we find we are looking to these things for satisfaction and fulfillment in life, then this may be an indication that a subtle form of cistern construction is going on. Let us return to the fountain of living waters before we discover too late in life that our self-made reservoirs were broken cisterns.

Let us apply God's broken cistern message to our own nation. This country was founded on the premise that we were a nation under God. Although the principle of separation between church and state was realized right from the beginning, the idea of separation between God and state was never envisioned. God was recognized as sovereign over the state as well as the church and as the One "from Whom all blessings flow." But the age of secularism has come and changed the mind-set of this nation. God has been largely banned from the sphere of the state and relegated to the sphere of the church only. Not only is His sovereignty over the state denied, but His very existence is questioned and doubted by many. Our nation has turned from the fountain of living waters to the cisterns of secular humanism. These self-made cisterns of human "freedom" in every area from sex to science are defiant slaps in the face of God. Our nation has condoned the construction of cisterns which deny God and the teaching of the Bible.

But the cisterns of secular humanism are broken cisterns. Regardless of how much so-called freedom is offered from any one of these self-made cisterns, complete fulfillment and satisfaction cannot be obtained apart from the fountain of living waters. Lapping the stagnant waters of these cisterns not only fails to quench our spiritual thirst, but ultimately it leads to the poison of dehumanization. Look, for example, at the man-made cistern of evolution compared to the biblical teaching of the noble beginnings of mankind, created in the image of God. Look also at the broken marriages and families that have resulted from drinking at the humanistic cistern of sexual freedom.

God gave the nation of Judah chance after chance to return to the Lord but they turned farther away. In terms of the illustration, Jeremiah 2:18 indicates that instead of turning back to the fountain of living waters from the broken cisterns with no water, they turned to the river waters of the Nile and the Euphrates. In other words, they looked more and more to the gods and government of Egypt and Assyria for protection and provision rather than to the faithful God of Israel. As a result, the Lord declared that His people would reap what they had sown (verse 19). And so the nation of Judah was conquered and taken away into slavery to Babylon (on the Euphrates) where they drank the bitter waters of their own choosing. The survivors who were left in the land of Israel ran away to Egypt against the explicit counsel of Jeremiah and there they died by the waters of the Nile. (See Jeremiah 42–44.)

How foolish to be involved in the evil of hewing cisterns! The consequences of such rebellion are just as serious and sure today as they were twenty-five hundred years ago for the nation of Judah. Whether it be a nation that turns away from God to the cisterns of secular humanism or even a Christian who looks for spiritual satisfaction and fulfillment apart from the Lord Himself, the Bible decrees that the sower will reap what he sows (Galatians 6:7). Why not avoid all the trouble and thirst, and drink forever at the fountain of living waters!

26

The Way of Escape

1 Corinthians 10:13   No temptation (or trial) has overtaken you but such as is common to man; and God is faithful, who will not allow you to be tempted (or tried) beyond what you are able, but with the temptation (or trial) will provide the way of escape also, that you may be able to endure it.

Suppose you are trapped on the second floor of a burning building, and there is no way out except to jump from a window. You are foolish if you don't take this way of escape. The leaping experience might be very painful, but a broken leg is nothing compared to being burned alive! Suppose you are being chased through the African bush by a lion. When all hope seems gone, you notice a ranger station. You are downright stupid if you don't run to the safety and help of the ranger. To take this way of escape is not to admit weakness and defeat—it is a matter of life instead of death. Suppose you are on a luxury liner that is just beginning to sink. Even before the ship shows the slightest sign of going down, the command to get into the lifeboats is given. You are very shortsighted if you don't avail yourself of this way of escape. Yes, it will mean leaving the fun-in-the-sun pleasure of the cruise. And it takes courage to commit yourself to the sea in a small lifeboat. But how much better it is to be saved before it is too late than to be caught helpless with the way of escape closed.

Certainly no one involved in any one of the hypothetical situations described above would turn away from the way of escape. Let's hope not! But think now of these cases as illustrations of spiritual realities. Is it not true that many people do not avail themselves of the way of escape when it comes to the salvation of their souls? Many who have realized their lost condition and have even been concerned about the destiny of their souls are reluctant to take the way of escape provided for them. How sad that people refuse the way of escape that God has promised in Christ!

These three illustrations of the way of escape have an application for believers as well as unbelievers. In fact, 1 Corinthians 10:13, which mentions "the way of escape," is addressed to Christians. The way of escape mentioned in this Scripture is not in reference to our eternal salvation. It has to do with our walk, or way of life, as believers. Notice that the way of escape is from a temptation (or trial) that has come upon us. How often we growing Christians are involved in situations which result in some sin or spiritual loss in our lives because we did not avail ourselves of the way of escape which God provided. As in the three illustrations, taking the way of escape to avoid spiritual failure or ruin may be very painful at times; or it may mean that the uninformed observer reads our actions as a sign of weakness; or it may mean separation from the things which are very pleasurable to our bodies and minds.

The important point to remember from 1 Corinthians 10:13 is that "the way of escape" is a wonderful promise that God has given to growing Christians. In fact, it is one of three very special promises or teachings that are contained in this verse. All three of these truths have to do with the subject of temptation. What about this word "temptation"? The first thought that usually comes to our minds when we read the word "temptation" is the idea of some kind of enticement to sin. However, the word translated "temptation" in the New Testament can also mean "trial" or "test." That is why the words "or trial" have been inserted after the word "temptation" in our text above. When this word occurs in the New Testament, the context will generally determine whether the meaning of the word is "solicitation to evil" or "trial." For example, in James 1 this word occurs in both verses 2 and 13. In verse 2, the obvious meaning is "trial," while in verse 13 the obvious meaning is "solicitation to evil." Now in 1 Corinthians 10:13 it appears that both these ideas are in view. Notice that the context concerns the children of Israel as they wandered in the wilderness for forty years. Here they not only yielded to temptations which caused them to commit immorality and idolatry, but they were tested by God to see what was "in their heart." (See Deuteronomy 8.) Therefore when we apply 1 Corinthians 10:13 to ourselves, as the Corinthians were exhorted to do, we should recognize that the promises made here have to do not only with what we normally consider temptation but also with any trial that we may be called upon to face.

The first truth concerning temptation or trial in verse 13 is the assurance that we are not unique. The temptations and trials which we face are those that befall all mankind. We can't excuse ourselves by saying, "No person has ever had this temptation before!" or, "No one has ever had to go through the trial that I'm going through!" This Scripture will not allow that kind of reasoning. Our trials are not greater than those that other Christians have had to face. Just to know that others have been in similar circumstances before us, and many have weathered the storm, should be an encouragement to us.

The second promise or truth in verse 13 is that God will never allow us to be tempted or tested beyond our abilities. We will never be swept away by an overpowering temptation. We are never the victims of circumstance. We are never put in an impossible situation. We can never say, "I couldn't resist!" or, "The devil made me do it!" The temptation or trial will never be too heavy, regardless of the time or pressure involved. God knows our abilities and limitations, and He sovereignly sets the bounds of any test given us and any "solicitation to evil" that Satan throws at us. (See Job 1 and 2 in this connection, and particularly the concept of the "hedge" in 1:10.) Let us remember this promise when we are in the middle of a temptation or test.

The third promise is the guarantee of the way of escape. Along with the temptation or trial will come the ability to endure. This is the basic idea behind "the way of escape." It is not the idea of a way to avoid dealing with the problem or of making it disappear.

No, it is the idea of escape through endurance. But the ability and means to endure are available. That is the promise! In terms of the three illustrations used before, the burning building will not suddenly stop burning, but the open window will be there; the pursuing lion will not suddenly drop dead or disappear, but the ranger station will be there; the sinking ship will not miraculously mend itself, but the lifeboats will be there. When faced with temptation or trial, let us look for the open windows and the ranger stations and the lifeboats that God promises will be there to enable us to endure.

The promise of the way of escape is not a promise that the way out will be easy to follow. Taking the way of escape to avoid spiritual failure may involve hurt, as pointed out in the illustration of the burning building. But the hurt of broken bones may leave the life preserved for further service and glory for Christ. Consider the case of the Christian girl who, because of the explicit teaching of Scripture in 2 Corinthians 6:14, purposes in her heart not to marry the nice non-Christian guy who proposes to her. She will experience hurt and pain as she severs the relationship, but her life will be spared from future spiritual loss. Her decision to say no may not be easy, but there will be the way of escape to enable her to endure. It may come as an opportunity to change locations. It may come through meeting new Christian friends. The way of escape may be provided just by seeing or hearing of the unfortunate results that come from an unequal yoke in the life of an aquaintance. The way out may even be provided by a renewed conviction of the authority of God's Word, as she yields herself more to the control of the Holy Spirit.

To take the way of escape may seem at times to be a sign of weakness or defeat, but this is not necessarily true. The Christian couple, for example, seeking godly counsel because of problems in their relationship, is not showing signs of defeat any more than the person running to the ranger for help in escaping the lion. It is not a sign of weakness for a couple to escape from a threatening situation by running to the safety and security of a Christian counselor. This is very often the way of escape that God provides. In fact, for us not to seek the aid of a mature Christian counselor may result in our being "mauled by the lion." Remember that "the devil prowls about like a roaring lion, seeking someone to devour" (1 Peter 5:8).

The way of escape will sometimes involve turning away from the pleasure cruise ship and committing oneself to the hardships of the lifeboat. Think of the Christian college student who realizes that he is being pressured into a pattern of life that is just one big selfish pleasure trip. It takes more than a little commitment to separate oneself from this lifestyle and get involved with a Christian fellowship group on campus, or a small Bible church in the community. These "lifeboats" are not always the most inviting and glamourous, but they are the ways of escape that God provides and promises will be there. This application is certainly appropriate to more Christians than just college students. Many growing Christians find themselves being drawn into the pleasures of this world. This world system is a sinking ship. (See 1 John 2:17.) Why risk spiritual shipwreck while the way of escape is still available? Putting the Lord first in our way of living is not only obedience, but it may very well be "the way of escape" from future spiritual ruin.

27

Is Euthanasia a Euphemism?

> *Exodus 20:13*   You shall not murder.
> *Exodus 4:11*   And the LORD said to him, "Who has made man's mouth? Or who makes him dumb or deaf, or seeing or blind? Is it not I, the LORD?"
> *Job 2:10b*   "Shall we indeed accept good from God and not accept adversity?" In all this Job did not sin with his lips.
> *Deuteronomy 32:39*   "See now that I, I am He, And there is no god besides Me; It is I who put to death and give life. I have wounded, and it is I who heal; And there is no one who can deliver from My hand."
> *Ecclesiastes 3:1-2*   There is an appointed time for everything. And there is a time for every event under heaven—A time to give birth, and a time to die.

A euphemism is an agreeable or pleasant sounding expression that is substituted for an expression that may be offensive or provoking or unpleasant. Senior citizen is a euphemism for old age. Husky or full-figured are euphemisms for overweight or fat. Souvenir hunting is a euphemism for vandalism. Is euthanasia also a euphemism?

The word euthanasia literally means "good death" or "easy death." Euthanasia is the act of killing, for reasons of mercy, persons that are hopelessly sick or handicapped or injured. Consequently, euthanasia is more commonly known as "mercy killing." But is killing for reasons of mercy somehow less than killing? Isn't mercy killing just a euphemism for murder?

The issue of euthanasia is contemporary within our culture. Advances in medical technology have enabled us to preserve and prolong human life far longer than in the past, and consequently all kinds of difficult questions are being raised. Why, for example, shouldn't an old person be allowed and even persuaded to die with dignity? What's the point of dragging on the earthly existence of the elderly who have already enjoyed full, happy, and useful lives? What about hopelessly ill or injured persons of any age? Why not mercifully pull the plug and bypass a great deal of needless pain and suffering? Why prolong the life of an infant who is born with major physical handicaps or severe mental retardation? Wouldn't a lot of expense and years of anxiety be avoided if such newborns were just permitted or even "helped" to die a natural death?

These questions are just a sampling of the many formidable and troublesome questions in this uncharted area that need answers today. We can see that euthanasia is not an issue with quick and easy answers for the Christian. In fact, euthanasia is probably one of the most difficult issues facing the Christian community today. What are the biblical answers?

You will not find the word euthanasia listed in a

biblical concordance, but there are certainly scriptural principles in God's all-sufficient Word that apply to this complicated matter. The five Scriptures listed above give some guidelines and also some boundaries for our thinking on this issue. On the one hand, the Bible obviously teaches that to willfully and deliberately terminate an innocent human life is wrong. To do so would be to break the sixth commandment: "You shall not murder" (Exodus 20:13). But what about human life that is "less than normal"? God's response to Moses in Exodus 4:11 is a strong statement showing that the presence of some kind of physical handicap does not in any way lower the value of human life. We read here that God has purposely allowed certain handicapped persons to be born and live. Exodus 4:11 therefore logically condemns the putting to death of handicapped newborns or handicapped individuals of any age. The reason why God made some "dumb or deaf or seeing or blind" is not the question here. (See John 9:1-3 for one answer.) The point here is that to deliberately end the life of a so-called less than normal person is to kill, even if it seems more compassionate or efficient in some cases.

But what about the person who is going through extreme suffering or experiencing intense pain due to illness or injury? Isn't euthanasia justified in such a case? The book of Job gives us some guidelines here. Job is well-known for his patient endurance through much suffering. Some insight into the extent of Job's horrible and painful physical condition can be seen in Job 2:7-8; 7:5; 13:28; 30:16-18,30. Wouldn't an easy and merciful death have been better for Job than the continuous, torturous pain of worms eating away at his body? Even Job's wife suggested that it would be better to curse God and die than to go on living in such a miserable and painful condition. Job himself certainly wanted to die. He longed for death (Job 3:20-22). But Job chose to endure. His response was, "Shall we indeed accept good from God and not accept adversity?" Job recognized that his suffering was by divine permission and purpose. The fact that the end of Job 2:10 states that Job did not sin in all of this leaves no doubt that Job's analysis of the situation was correct. His decision, to endure the suffering rather than have his life taken before God's time, was right. Again, the reason why God allows suffering is not the question here. (Read the whole book of Job for part of that answer.) Nor is the question of using painkilling drugs before us here. (Proverbs 31:6 would seem to justify the medicinal use of drugs for relief of pain.) The conclusion here is that to mercifully terminate a life because of suffering or pain is not justified. It is the wrongful taking of human life. It is murder.

Now on the other hand, the Bible just as clearly teaches that God does have the right to terminate life. Whether in judgment or in mercy, or for some other sovereign purpose, God is never wrong in taking a human life. Deuteronomy 32:39 states that God puts to death and gives life. (See also 1 Samuel 2:6 and Psalm 90:3.) The giving and taking of human life are the prerogatives of God alone. It is true that God has delegated the responsibility of capital punishment to human governments (see Genesis 9:6), and there are the legitimate questions concerning just wars and self-defense. These matters certainly have biblical grounds for discussion but are not the issue before us now. The focus of the argument here is that while we do not have the right to take innocent life, God very definitely does have that right. Ecclesiastes 3:1-2 goes further and says that there is a "time to die." God not only has the right to take a life but He has a time appointed when He takes that life.

The whole point of Ecclesiastes 3:1-8 is that all the events of life are divinely appointed. Human responsibility, moreover, is also in view in the passage, as a matter of our duty in light of these divinely appointed times. When it is time to be silent (verse 7) we may be silent or make the mistake of opening our big mouths. When it is a divinely appointed time to weep (verse 4), as commanded in Romans 12:15, we may weep or we may sin by not being concerned. Man has a responsibility in all the areas mentioned (including capital punishment or just war, which seems to be the focus of Ecclesiastes 3:3), to be sensitive to God's appointed times and act accordingly. Along this line of reasoning, then, could we not make a mistake and prevent the death of an individual whose divinely appointed "time to die" has arrived? Should we use every new and extraordinary medical technique available to prolong biological life as long as possible? Is there not a line between protecting the act of living and prolonging the act of dying? If taking a life before God's appointed time of death is wrong, is not perpetuating a life beyond God's appointed time of death also wrong?

But how do we know when God's time to die has arrived for an individual? This is the basic issue for the Christian. In other words, euthanasia by definition should not be an issue for the growing Christian. We've seen that euthanasia or mercy killing is wrong according to biblical teaching. It is a euphemism for killing or murder. But preventing death by perpetuating a life that God is taking is really another matter. It is true that there is some overlap here with so-called passive euthanasia. However, it is probably best to think of not perpetuating life as a separate issue, because in many cases of passive euthanasia something could and should have been done for the dying instead of precipitating death by doing nothing.

Unfortunately, the situation is usually not black and white for decision making. An infant born without a brain or a decapitated accident victim are obvious cases where the time to die has arrived, and using life support systems to keep the bodies "alive" (which is possible) would be wrong. However, most situations are much more complex and many factors must be taken into account. The request of the terminal cancer patient, the living will of the permanently unconscious individual, the reasonable hope of recovery of some rational capability for the infant or for the accident victim with severe brain damage, the possibility of a miracle cure, are just some of the particulars that must be considered and weighed before a decision is reached. It goes without saying that Christians involved in situations such as these are obligated to pray that God's will would be revealed as well as carried out. And in all cases, Christian love and care should be given to the patient of any age as we seek to stay within biblical boundaries and follow biblical guidelines in reference to the dying.

28

Only Five Loaves
and Two Fish

Matthew 14:16-18 But Jesus said to them,
"They do not need to go away; you give them
something to eat!" And they said to Him, "We
have here only five loaves and two fish." And
He said, "Bring them here to Me."
*Read the complete account in Matthew 14,
Mark 6, Luke 9, and John 6.*

Growing Christians are constantly surrounded
by and even bombarded with the needs of others.
There are crying physical and spiritual needs all
around us. The physical needs are not only in far-off
places where political unrest, earthquakes, floods, and
other natural disasters take many lives and leave
hundreds homeless. The spiritual needs are not only
on foreign mission fields or in the ghettos of distant
cities. To be sure, there are great needs in all of these
far-away areas, and we growing Christians have a responsibility to help meet these needs. We do it by

prayer and financial support—and by direct involvement wherever and whenever possible. There are many opportunities for us to help meet these needs through relief efforts and missionary endeavors around the world. But we also have a responsibility to meet the needs at home. Too often we excuse ourselves from the close-to-home needs because we gave a little time to some missionary project at church or a little money to some Christian organization which sent out an appeal by form letter. Again, let us stress that we must not neglect our responsibility to support worthwhile ministries. But we must ask ourselves if we are doing anything about the needs immediately around us. There are many physical and spiritual needs right in our own backyard: our school or college, our place of employment, our neighborhood, our church. In fact, when we take the blinders off we find that there are so many needs around us that we don't know where to begin. The problems sometimes seem so gigantic and hopeless and complicated that we get discouraged and end up doing little or nothing. So many needs! What can we do? What should we do?

The answers to those two important questions above are given to us in Jesus' miracle of feeding the five thousand. You see, the miracles of our Lord Jesus were never just arbitrary, spur of the moment bursts of raw, supernatural power. The miracles of Christ were designed to teach as well as to authenticate His deity. The miracles were always planned and purposeful demonstrations of the power of God. (See John 6:6 in this connection.) The how-to of meeting needs is one of the great teachings of the miracle of the feeding of the five thousand.

In order to appreciate the teaching of this well-known miracle of the Lord Jesus, let us first examine the setting of the miracle. Jesus had taken His disciples away from the exhausting demands of their ministry for a little rest and relaxation (Mark 6:7, 30-32). We see here that the principle of periodic retreats is definitely a biblical principle for the Christian servant. The Lord knows that we can't burn the candle at both ends, so He provides those times of rest and relaxation. This important principle of meeting needs must be kept in mind, especially by the Christian workaholic. Most growing Christians do not have this problem, however. Christian "relaxaholics" need to observe that the retreat did not last very long. No sooner had they arrived at the retreat center than the needy crowd showed up. Immediately the Lord began to minister to their many physical and spiritual needs (Luke 9:11). Apparently the disciples just stood around and watched for a while. Maybe they were even a little annoyed because their vacation had ended so abruptly. In any case, as evening approached, the disciples suggested to Jesus that He send the hungry crowd away to find food and lodging for the night. They certainly didn't expect the Lord's response to them: "You give them something to eat!"

We can imagine the disciples' thinking and reasoning at this point. "Hey, wait a minute, Lord. This isn't our responsibility! These people came out here on their own without any food or forethought. Now they can live with the consequences of their shortsighted decisions. Why should we get involved? Look at the magnitude of the need! We just don't have the resources. Besides, who invited them to our retreat, anyway?" It's very easy to see ourselves in all of this, isn't it? That fellow student who is messing up her life should know better. Why should I try to help her? That guy I work with is always getting himself into financial difficulties through his own shortsightedness. There's no way I'm going to get involved in his dilemma! My resources are too limited, anyway. That neighbor of mine has so many problems. If I follow that love-your-neighbor-as-yourself principle, I'll never have any time for myself. In view of the setting of this miracle, our Lord's statement, "Give them something to eat," certainly rules out a lot of our excuses. We do have a definite responsibility to meet the needs of people around us, regardless of our vacation plans or the magnitude of the need or the question of who's at fault. This second principle must be kept in balance with the first principle. Let's not burn out, but let's not cop out, either!

Another principle which this miracle teaches is, "Give what you have." We are not expected to give what we don't have, but we are expected to give what we do have. When the disciples could round up only five loaves and two fish, the Lord didn't tell them to be ashamed of themselves or to quit goldbricking! But neither did He tell them to forget His command to feed the multitude, even though they could come up with only five loaves and two fish. Even though this was hardly enough to feed themselves, let alone the multitude, the disciples were expected to give what they had to meet the need. The Lord takes on Himself the responsibility of multiplication. Our responsibility is to give what we have to Him—no more but no less. The little we have can meet the greatest need when given to Christ and then multiplied by Him. Think of it! More than five thousand (possibly twelve thousand or more, counting women and children) were fed with only five loaves of bread and two fish—multiplied! How many spiritually hungry people needing Christ are in your neighborhood or on your campus or in your place of employment? Did you say several thousand? What do you have to give? Did you say you have only a small stammering testimony for Christ? What an opportunity for God to work a miracle! Give what you have. Your small but faithful and consistent testimony can affect the entire block or campus or company in an almost unbelievable way for our Lord.

In light of the teaching of this miracle, that God can do wonders with our "five loaves and two fish," why aren't we seeing more of the spiritual and physical needs around us met? Maybe it's because we are not giving all that we have. Are we like the little boy who gave his whole lunch (John 6:9)? Or are we holding out by giving two or three loaves and one fish and keeping the rest for ourselves? What about our time and abilities, and what about our goals for the future? Remember that the boy was hungry like the rest of the multitude. And remember that he had no idea how the Lord was going to use his lunch or that he would end up getting as much as he wanted to eat (John 6:11-12). He was not forced to give anything, but he willingly gave his whole brown bag to the Lord. Where is my brown bag? Am I still clinging to my five loaves and two fish to meet my own needs and wants, or have I turned them all over to the Lord? As in the case of the little boy, we can be sure that God will continue to meet our needs as we work with Him in meeting the needs of others.

Perhaps another reason why we're not meeting more of spiritual and physical needs around us is that we don't bring our five loaves and two fish to the Lord for multiplication. We may recognize the needs and our responsibilities to meet these needs, and we may try with all of our five and two to meet these needs. But unless we follow the Lord's command, "Bring them to Me" (Matthew 14:18), we will not see too many mouths fed. We must literally depend on God to multiply our meager contribution. We just are not capable of producing a miracle in our own strength. Many growing Christians have tried and ended up discouraged, disheartened, and skeptical. But God is able. Watch the ways in which your dedicated efforts to meet the needs of just a few fellow students or neighbors or work contacts will ripple out miraculously in blessing to many others. And what a blessing to ourselves when we really catch this principle of meeting needs and wait by faith in excited anticipation for the multiplication miracle! Here, then, is a further teaching of this great miracle. The giver of five loaves and two fish will always be blessed along with the receiver. In fact, we will end up with more than we had when we started. Notice that each of the disciples received a basket containing more than five loaves and two fish (Mark 6:43). God will always resupply our resources for the further meeting of needs.

The Lord Jesus could have provided bread for the multitude in any number of different ways. As God, He could have precipitated manna from the skies as He did in the Old Testament. But He chose the option of multiplying a little boy's lunch. Why? Because He wanted to teach His disciples, then and now, a few lessons about meeting the needs around them with only five loaves and two fish.

29

Betrayed

1 Corinthians 11:23-24   For I received from the Lord that which I also delivered to you, that the Lord Jesus in the night in which He was betrayed took bread; and when He had given thanks, He broke it, and said, "This is My body, which is for you; do this in remembrance of Me."
John 13:18   I do not speak of all of you. I know the ones I have chosen; but it is that the Scripture may be fulfilled, HE WHO EATS MY BREAD HAS LIFTED UP HIS HEEL AGAINST ME.
Psalm 41:9   Even my close friend, in whom I trusted, who ate my bread, has lifted up his heel against me.

Have you ever been betrayed by a close friend—someone you completely trusted? Such an experience is beyond emotional grasp for many of us. We all know how it feels when people take advantage of us or when unprincipled individuals step on us. But to be betrayed by a trusted friend hurts much more.

When we think of the suffering of a dedicated and faithful wife who is betrayed by her husband or an innocent young child who is betrayed by parents, we can begin to comprehend the emotional hurt that comes with betrayal. This kind of suffering is deeper and more grievous than physical suffering. Usually there are limits to physical pain, but there is continual mental and emotional anguish associated with personal betrayal.

Our Lord Jesus was betrayed. He was betrayed by a close "friend." He was betrayed on the special night that was meant to be a time of intimate fellowship between Himself and His trusted companions. Jesus knew full well that this betrayal would lead to His death by crucifixion the next day. (See Luke 9:22-23 and John 13:1-2,11.) Imagine how we would feel, on the night before our death, if we knew our lives were to be taken from us—in the prime of life. What would we be thinking if we knew that our violent death would be brought about by the betrayal of a close friend? Our feelings would probably range from helplessness and fear to a mixture of bitterness and anger. Our thoughts would likely include ideas of revenge or notions of recanting our faith and certainly plans for running away while there was still time. But all of these thoughts and feelings were foreign to our Lord. 1 Corinthians 11:23-24 informs us that He gave thanks on the night in which He was betrayed. The Lord was not thinking of preserving His life for Himself but of giving His life for us. He was not going to run away in fear. He would persevere to the end and finish His special work. We gain a greater appreciation of the magnitude of our Lord's courage and commitment and endurance, as well as His incredible love for us, as we remember that the events of Good Friday took place against the black background of His betrayal.

The extent of the treachery of our Lord's betrayer is seen in John 13. During the course of the Last Supper, Jesus told His disciples that one of them would betray Him. In verse 18, the Lord introduced the subject with a quotation from Psalm 41: "He who eats my bread has lifted up his heel against me." Soon after this statement the Lord privately indicated to Peter and John that Judas was the betrayer. Judas! Who would have suspected Judas? He was the appointed and trusted treasurer of the group. Maybe impetuous Peter, but certainly not responsible Judas! Religious artists usually portray Judas as a sly and crafty individual in appearance, but that is not the picture of Judas that emerges from the Bible. His unbelief and his traitorous character were amazingly masked right to the end. Over a three year period he was able to pilfer money from the others without arousing the least suspicion (John 12:6). Even after going to the authorities, bargaining for the blood money and deliberately plotting to betray Jesus, Judas still posed as a model disciple. Along with the rest of the disciples at the Passover, Judas asked, "Surely it is not I, Rabbi?" (See Matthew 26:15,16,25; Mark 14:19, and John 13:2.) In John 13:26 we learn that Judas readily responded to Christ's friendly gesture of sharing food during the meal without the slightest misgiving or indication of the base designs that were in his heart. The gesture of Jesus, as the host, giving a portion to Judas, one of the guests, was an indication of honor in that culture and thus further heightens the hypocrisy of Judas. And when Judas left the upper room to do his heinous work, some of the other disciples thought that Jesus was sending him on a responsible mission for the group (John 13:29). What an extraordinary cover-up Judas was able to pull off for his outrageous treachery!

In light of these details we stand amazed and awed at the patience and gentleness of our Savior as well as His willing submission to humiliation. The Lord was not fooled by Judas. He knew the hearts of all men (John 2:24-25). He knew from the beginning that Judas was the betrayer (John 6:64,71). And yet for three years the Lord Jesus graciously tolerated Judas, a man of whom Christ Himself said, "It would have been good for that man if he had not been born" (Matthew 26:24). Think of all the times of joy and sorrow that Jesus shared with His own—and Judas. Think of the long hours that our Lord spent teaching His close followers—among them Judas. Think of the supernatural power and authority that Christ conferred on the twelve—including Judas (Matthew 10:1). Think of how the Lord washed all the disciples' feet (John 13:5,12). Think of the many typical embraces that the Lord must have shared with Judas. (Since the kiss was probably the normal greeting between Jesus and His disciples, Judas would have felt confident that it could be used as the betraying signal.) Finally, think of how the Lord Jesus endured that final embrace and kiss of betrayal from Judas (Mark 14:43-46). How it must have deeply hurt the tender, gentle, and sensitive soul of the Lord to look directly into the eyes of His betrayer and say, "Judas, are you betraying the Son of Man with a kiss?" (Luke 22:48).

Why? Why such long-suffering and tolerance on the part of Christ? Why did the Lord show such willing submission to humiliation? There were probably a number of reasons, all of which involved the working out of God's sovereign plans for man's salvation. For example, the cruel and sinful depravity of man was clearly shown, not only in the mockery and spitting and scourging by the *pagan* Roman soldiers, and the rejection and despising by the *religious* Jews, but also the betrayal by one of the *disciples*. In addition, we certainly have before us a remarkable demonstration of the way the Lord deals with each one of us. What incredible long-suffering the Lord has shown toward *us!* How long did He put up with our hearts of rebellion before we turned to Him for salvation? How much humiliation have we, as Christians, brought upon the One who gave His life for us? How much hurt have we caused the heart of our Savior through our actions—or our inaction? How many times have we hypocritically compromised in the faith and "betrayed" our Lord for literally less than thirty pieces of this world's silver? Consider the deadly sins of pride, covetousness, jealously, ambition, and willfulness that lie in the depths of our own hearts (Jeremiah 17:9). Surely we must agree that but for the amazing grace of God, every one of us could have taken the place of Judas.

Psalm 41 gives us further insight into the betrayal and the humiliation of our Lord. In this psalm, David is reflecting on the time when his son, Absalom, seized the kingdom and usurped the throne of Israel. David fled from Jerusalem with his loyal followers, but his close friend and trusted counselor, Ahithophel, betrayed David and sided with Absalom. He even told Absalom how to go about destroying David! (Read the story in 2 Samuel 15–18.) The fact that our Lord quoted Psalm 41:9 proves that Ahithophel prophetically portrayed Judas. It is noteworthy in this connection that Ahithophel, like Judas, hanged himself when he realized that his counsel to the enemies of David had been overruled (2 Samuel 17:23). It is also significant that when our Lord applied this Scripture to Judas, He did not quote the first part of the verse. Jesus left out, "Even my close friend in whom I trusted," for obvious reasons. By quoting the second half of Psalm 41:9, the Lord Jesus indicated that He was keenly aware of the hatefulness and the blackness of the treachery before Him. As Ahithophel deceptively posed beneath the shelter of Eastern hospitality and sat at David's own table, so did Judas at the Lord's table. As Ahithophel disgracefully partook of his master's bread, so did Judas at the Passover feast and institution of the Lord's Supper (Luke 22:19-21). As Ahithophel shamefully betrayed the king and plotted to assassinate him, so did Judas, with such deceitful candor. As Ahithophel viciously lifted up his heel and "kicked" his lord, so did Judas, with sudden and shocking brutality, in the most infamous betrayal the world has ever known.

As we reflect on the betrayal of our Lord, may our hearts go out to Him in more love and devotion for all that He suffered. His road to the cross for our salvation was paved with indescribable sorrows. May we also examine our hearts and lives for areas in which we are guilty of bringing humiliation to the name of Christ. May our all-too-frequent "betrayals" of our Savior for worldly profit or popularity be brought to an abrupt end. May we, with His promised help, take action to live out a clear profession of our faith in Christ Jesus our Lord.

30

The Joy of Living

Ecclesiastes 11:9–12:1   Rejoice, young
man, during your childhood, and let your
heart be pleasant during the days of your
young manhood. And follow the impulses of
your heart and the desires of your eyes. Yet
know that God will bring you to judgment for
all these things. So remove vexation from
your heart and put away pain from your body,
because childhood and the prime of life are
fleeting. Remember also your Creator in the
days of your youth.
Read all of Ecclesiastes.

Balance in the Christian life is not always easy
and it is certainly not automatic for the growing Christian. There are always the temptations to go off on
certain do-your-own-thing tangents. And there are always the extreme positions that tend to draw you to
one side or another. Then, of course, there are those
"helpful" Christians that keep telling you what they
think you ought to be doing or not doing. Maintaining

a proper balance is difficult in the middle of all these tensions and conflicting opinions. Having fun and enjoying life is one of the most difficult areas in which to achieve balance as a Christian. If we're having too much fun and feeling too happy all the time, other Christians may accuse us of not taking life seriously. We may even put ourselves on a guilt trip because of this supposed over-indulgence in fun and happiness! But then if we're too sober and too serious all the time, our Christian friends begin preaching put-on-a-smile messages at us. And in all seriousness, life may indeed begin to drag for us with no excitement and nothing to look forward to. You just can't seem to win! Achieving a proper balance in this area of living is hard. And the problem is not just in the mind. There are the very real dangers of self-indulgence on the one hand and discouragement or depression on the other if the right attitude toward having fun and enjoying life is not held and practiced.

The book of Ecclesiastes may seem like an unlikely place to find guidelines for the proper attitude toward fun and happiness in life. Many Christians who read this book of Scripture for the very first time come away with somewhat of a depressed feeling because of the recurring "all is vanity" theme. However, Ecclesiastes has more to share than just the idea that everything is vanity or meaningless. In fact, this book has so much to say about happiness and delight in life that the theme of Ecclesiastes could be considered, "The Joy of Living." Now it is certainly true that Ecclesiastes is not the most simple and straightforward portion of Scripture to understand. For this reason there have been various approaches to the interpretation to this part of God's Word throughout the history of the church. However, after the book has been read through several times, the overall message of Ecclesiastes seems to come through loud and clear. It is as follows: without God in the picture, life is meaningless; with God in the picture, there can be joy in living. If God is not acknowledged and taken into account, then life "under the sun" is just one big zero. It doesn't matter what you are involved in: studies, styles, sex, or stocks (Ecclesiastes 1:12–2:11). Ultimately, without God, all of life is vanity—empty, futile, and meaningless. One has to be blind to miss this aspect of the message from Ecclesiastes. But surely the corollary is also found in this book of Scripture. When God is acknowledged and reverenced and obeyed, life becomes meaningful; the believer can actually find happiness and enjoyment in living. In fact, Ecclesiastes tells us that this is one of God's gifts to man from His own hand, a reward to those who fear the Lord. (See Ecclesiastes 2:24-26; 3:12-13; 5:18-20; 9:7-9.)

Although God allows His children to find happiness and joy in living, it does not follow that we will therefore understand life completely or fathom all of God's ways. The Holy Spirit is careful to stress this point several times throughout the book of Ecclesiastes. For instance, in chapter 3:10-11 note that God has purposely made man finite in reference to comprehending eternal matters. But even though man is limited in his grasp of this universe and cannot figure out all of life's questions, the believer can rest in the knowledge that the Lord is in control of His creation and has an appointed and appropriate time for everything (3:1-11). Furthermore (3:12-13), we can enjoy the short life that God has given us on earth, in spite of life's enigmas and seeming contradictions and apparent meaninglessness. It is not wrong to laugh and have fun, to enjoy life and seek pleasure, as long as God and His guidelines for happiness are brought into the picture.

This, then, is the overall message of Ecclesiastes. All texts within the book should be read and understood in the context of this overall theme. Before we mention some of the guidelines for happiness that God has given us, one other point about the interpretation of this book of Scripture should be stressed. Sometimes Solomon, the inspired author of this book, writes from the perspective of the first part of the book's thesis, namely that without God in the picture, all is meaningless. When these verses are taken out of the surrounding context and isolated from the overall message of the book, it can sound like the Preacher (Ecclesiastes 1:1) is teaching untruth. For example, in chapter 3:19 we read that the fate of man and animals is the same, and that man has no advantage over the animal. Now we know from the rest of Scripture that the Bible does not teach this idea. But Ecclesiastes is not teaching such falsehood either. We don't have to look far in the surrounding context to see what is being taught here. Verse 17 clearly shows that the inspired teacher knows that man and animals are different and that man is going to be morally judged. But God has purposely tested man (3:18) by letting it appear that the destiny of men and beasts is the same. Only by revelation can we know the truth: that the spirit of man does indeed ascend upward in contrast to that of the beast (3:21). This truth is also taught explicitly in chapter 12:7. So be specially careful in Ecclesiastes and make sure that the so-called difficult passages are not pulled out of context and interpreted apart from the perspective of the inspired writer. See

Psalm 49:12,20 for a similar example from another inspired author.

Now what about those guidelines for enjoying life that God has included in Ecclesiastes? There are basically three, and they are listed together in the conclusion of the book (Ecclesiastes 12:13-14): Fear God, keep His commandments, and remember the coming judgment! These controls on our fun and pleasure do not just appear in the last two verses of the book, but pop up a number of times throughout Ecclesiastes. Besides the passages already listed, see chapter 5:1-7, 8:12-13, 11:9-10, and 12:1-7. In other words, you can "follow the impulses of your hearts and the desires of your eyes" (11:9a), but you must also remember the guideline of "know that God will bring you to judgment for all these things" (11:9b). You can live it up a little while you are young and have the chance (11:9-10) but you must "remember also your Creator" (12:1a). This will guard you from living it up too much! Remembering our Creator is especially important while we're young and in good health and have energies to dedicate, not just when we're old and falling apart (12:1b-7). So it's O.K. to have a fun time on a weekend away from studies. It's O.K. to be happy and lighthearted while we barbeque a steak dinner with our friends. And it's O.K. to take off the so-serious mask and laugh. It's O.K. to get into a line of work that you like. And it's O.K. to enjoy the pleasures of sex in marriage. All of these O.K.'s are gifts of God to man. But— fear God, keep His commandments, and remember that our lives will be judged or reviewed (2 Corinthians 5:10) for all our attitudes and actions. The Lord knows our weaknesses and how easily we're tempted to abuse His wonderful gifts. Let us follow the guidelines so that the good fun and games of life are properly controlled. Remember also that God may purposely bring times of sorrow, times of testing, and other less delightful times into our lives. Here the general attitude of being outwardly happy and enjoying life is certainly modified. Ecclesiastes takes these times into account, too. (See chapters 3:4 and 7:2-4, for example.)

Every book of Scripture must be understood in the light of the teaching of the whole Bible, and Ecclesiastes is no exception, of course. For the growing Christian, the application of the guidelines of Ecclesiastes concerning the enjoyment of life must further take into account New Testament revelation. The overall message of Ecclesiastes is not changed in the New Testament. See 1 Timothy 6:17, for instance, and note how life is to be enjoyed as long as God and His guidelines stay in the picture. However, we also know from New Testament teaching that a Christian now has the privilege of giving up, for the sake of Christ, certain of God's gifts to mankind. A Christian student, for example, may give up a good, fun-filled weekend away from school to help organize the Christian outreach program on campus. A Christian athlete may give up the benefits of a professional career in sports to serve the Lord more effectively as a leader of a struggling ministry or as the elder of a small church. A Christian young person may give up the joys of married life in order to give a life of undivided attention to the foreign mission field. Every growing Christian has the freedom to enjoy the rich supply of God's good gifts, but we also have the privilege of denying ourselves certain joys of life as the Lord calls us to particular areas of service for Him.

God is not a killjoy. The normal pattern of living

which He desires for us includes happiness and the enjoyment of the life He has given us. But there must be balance in this area of Christian life. Ecclesiastes, properly understood in the context of the whole Bible, gives us God's guidelines for living joyously.

31

Just Joseph

Matthew 1:18-19 Now the birth of Jesus
Christ was as follows. When His mother Mary
had been betrothed to Joseph, before they
came together she was found to be with child
by the Holy Spirit. And Joseph her husband,
being a [just] man, and not wanting to
disgrace her, desired to put her away secretly.
Read Matthew 1–2.

 W hat do you know about the Joseph who
stands in the background of the Christmas nativity
scenes? What kind of a man did God choose to be the
earthly father of our Lord? We know he was a carpenter
by vocation (Matthew 13:55), but what was he like in
character? Was he just an average believer like most
of us, or was he an outstanding man of God?

According to Matthew 1:19, Joseph was a *just* man.
He was a righteous man. Joseph was not perfect or
sinless, but his life was characterized by consistently
doing what was right before God. Joseph was not only

a good honest carpenter but he exhibited outstanding moral qualities in every area of his life. Even though the Bible does not contain a lot about this man, the virtuous character and moral excellence of Joseph emerge from the few verses that God has given us about him. As we study what the Bible has to say about "just Joseph," we should be challenged to follow his example.

Joseph was a man of *love*. We see his love demonstrated in his tender care and consideration of Mary, even under very difficult circumstances. Imagine Joseph's predicament when he found out that his beloved fiancée was pregnant. Mary's explanations about "angel announcements" and "Holy Spirit conception" were just too much to believe. With deep hurt and disappointment Joseph must have concluded that sometime during Mary's three-month visit to her cousin Elizabeth (Luke 1:56), she had been unfaithful to him. How could she have done this to the man who truly loved her? And then to not even confess and tell him the truth! She insisted that this was all of God and pleaded with him to understand. Joseph had never known such emotional stress and trauma and hurt!

At this point Joseph was left with two options. He loved God and he wanted to do what was right. According to God's law (Deuteronomy 22:23-24), Mary could have been put to death. Even if a public stoning was waived, at least she could have been denounced publicly. (This action would also have the effect of "protecting" Joseph's reputation.) But Joseph loved Mary, in spite of her apparent unfaithfulness to him. There was no desire in his heart for any kind of revenge. For Mary's sake he decided to keep things as quiet as possible and break the engagement privately.

Because Mary had not been proven guilty, he had the option of dispensing with his legal rights. Maybe he thought Mary could go back to stay with Elizabeth, who lived some distance away. She could have the baby there and avoid a very painful scandal in Nazareth. Joseph was a man of love and wanted to do the best for Mary—even when he thought she had betrayed him.

Do we show the same kind of love that Joseph exhibited? What is our reaction when we believe a Christian friend has wronged us or someone we're close to has deeply hurt us? Do we look for an opportunity to get back at that person? Are we filled with anger and bitterness? Do we run away from the scene of our hurt so that we can just forget everything? Or do we continue to love that Christian friend and try to do not only what's right by God's standards but also what's best for the person who has stepped on us? This kind of love is never easy, but it is possible. (See John 17:26.)

Joseph was also a man of *faith*. By this we mean that he was more than just a believer. "Just Joseph" lived and walked by faith in the living God. Faithful Joseph must have spent a long time in prayer as he considered what to do about Mary (Matthew 1:20). It wasn't that he didn't want to believe her story, but how could he have accepted such a fantasy? To believe such an incredible story would take gullibility, not faith. A virgin birth had never happened throughout the history of man—not even back in the miracle days of the prophets.

It was at this point that an angel from the Lord appeared to Joseph in a dream. The angel confirmed everything that Mary had shared with him. She had been faithful! The conception was of the Holy Spirit. Mary was the virgin of Isaiah's messianic prophecy (Matthew 1:23). Joseph's fiancée was going to be the mother of the long-awaited Messiah. And he was to be the earthly father of this Child and was to name Him Jesus. What unexpected good news! What unbelievable relief of soul! Joseph must have experienced reverent awe and ecstatic joy at the same time. He wasted no time in marrying Mary (verse 24)—concrete evidence of his faith in God. Can you imagine the beautiful and excited reunion of this godly couple?

The faith of Joseph should be an example for all of us. Notice that Joseph never questioned the angel or doubted the divine revelation given to him. Notice that the angel never questioned Joseph either. There was no rebuke for Joseph's conclusions about Mary. The Lord does not hold us responsible to believe the incredible without divine revelation. God is not looking for blind faith or gullible faith. He calls us to a reasonable faith—a faith which is grounded in His revealed Word. Joseph would certainly have known the Old Testament prophecies regarding the coming Messiah, and it was to these promises in the Word of God that the angel pointed Joseph (Matthew 1:21-23). As Joseph believed the angel because the message was grounded in Scripture, so we should believe and not doubt what God has plainly declared in His Word. Take the matter of our daily needs, for example. Do we worry about our security? Do we doubt God's ability to take care of us and meet our basic needs? To walk by reasonable faith means that we should not doubt or get anxious about our needs, because God has plainly declared that He Himself will provide "all these things" when we are seeking "His kingdom first" (Matthew 6:25-34).

Joseph was obviously a man of *obedience*. He readily obeyed the angel's command to take Mary as his wife, and that command was not easy to obey. Remember that Mary was at least three months pregnant at this time (Luke 1:56). By marrying Mary, Joseph was taking on himself all the accusations and stigma that were sure to surface shortly. In this connection, note the implication of the Jews' statement made some thirty years later: "We were not born of fornication" (John 8:41). But Joseph obeyed the angel's message, regardless of the consequences. A further example of Joseph's obedience is seen in Matthew 2:13-14. After Jesus' birth he was told by the angel to take his family to Egypt—quickly! Even though there were Jewish communities in Egypt at that time and even though God had provided the means for the trip through the gifts of the wise men, it was still quite an undertaking. To travel by donkey with Mary and young Jesus to an unfamiliar country at least three hundred miles away over wilderness terrain was not an easy task. But Joseph obeyed—promptly (Matthew 2:14). After they were settled in Egypt, however, Joseph was told to move again—back to Israel. Again Joseph obeyed without raising any questions about convenience or God's timetable.

Are we like Joseph in our obedience to the Lord's commands? Do we obey quickly, or do we practice partial and delayed obedience? What about the Lord's command to verbalize the gospel with our fellow neighbors and students that many of us find so hard to obey (Mark 16:15)? What about the area of our lusts, from which we are told to flee (2 Timothy 2:22)? Do we obey only when it's convenient and easy? What about the sins of criticizing others and complaining about circumstances? It's so convenient and easy to disobey in this area. Do we obey even when we don't understand what God is doing in our lives? Do we trust the Lord even when tragedy strikes and the future looks uncertain? (See Proverbs 3:5-6.) Joseph is a tremendous model to all of us of what it really means to trust and obey.

Finally, Joseph was a man of *patience*. We have already seen that he was not given to rash reactions. He thought through his course of action (Matthew 1:20). In Matthew 1:25 we are told that Joseph kept Mary a virgin until Jesus was born. Whether or not this was also a command from the angel we do not know. Certainly the divine/human nature of Christ would not have been affected in any way since conception had already taken place three months earlier. But perhaps in view of the prophecy that a virgin would conceive and bear a son, Joseph kept Mary a virgin until after the birth of Jesus. It doesn't take profound insight here to recognize that Joseph was a man of governed passions and disciplined patience.

The patience of Joseph needs to be practiced by Christians today. Impatience in the area of sexual desire has led to the downfall of many believers. If God gave Joseph patience in this area, He can give us patience as well. Remember, patience in all areas is part of the fruit of the Spirit who indwells and empowers every Christian. (See Galatians 5:22.)

During the Christmas season the figure of "just Joseph" stands in the background shadows of many nativity scenes. Let's be reminded to follow his example of love, faith, obedience, and patience.

32

The Finished Work of Christ

1 John 4:10   He loved us and sent His Son
to be the propitiation for our sins.
Ephesians 1:7   In Him we have redemption
through His blood.
2 Corinthians 5:18   Now all these things
are from God, who reconciled us to Himself
through Christ.

Many Christians shy away from a systematic
study of the doctrines of the Bible. After all, just the
mention of words like theology, Christology, pneumatology, anthropology, soteriology, ecclesiology, eschatology, and other tongue-twisters is enough to
scare anyone away. Surely a simple "what a friend we
have in Jesus" faith is all that any believer needs. Why
become concerned with all that heavy doctrine anyway? For one very good reason! Doctrine, by definition,
is what the Bible teaches, and knowing what the Bible
teaches is extremely important for the growing Christian. To know the Lord Jesus as our Savior and Friend

is wonderful, but there is much more to learn about our new life in Christ. God wants us to know what He has revealed about such things as the church, angels, heaven and hell, and future events, marriage and the family, and many other things. That's why He gave us a Bible that is a lot bigger than a pamphlet! Let's not let the big words scare us away. They are only a more formal way of categorizing what the Bible teaches about God (theology), Christ (Christology), the Holy Spirit (pneumatology), man (anthropology), salvation (soteriology), the church (ecclesiology), the future (eschatology), etc. Now it is true that the study of doctrine can be a boring at times because it does get pretty heavy in places. But stick with it, because coming to understand more and more of what God has revealed in Holy Scripture means coming to know more of God Himself.

The finished work of Christ is an area of doctrine that is often misunderstood or only partially understood by many Christians. This subject comes under the category of soteriology, that is, what the Scripture teaches about salvation. The Bible teaches that the salvation of mankind from the consequences of sin is both free and costly at the same time. On the one hand, salvation is a free gift to anyone who entrusts himself by faith to the Lord Jesus Christ as personal Savior. But on the other hand, salvation is very costly because it required the sacrificial death of the Son of God. It is this aspect of salvation that is referred to as the finished work of Christ. (See John 19:30.) It is not the miraculous birth of Christ nor the perfect life of Christ that is chiefly in view of this phrase. The finished work of Christ refers primarily to His death on the cross. That is where the judgment of God against our sin was endured by Christ, who became our Substitute in order to become our Savior. Jesus was not our Savior until He suffered and died for our sins on the cross.

The New Testament uses three key words to describe the finished work of Christ: propitiation, redemption, and reconciliation. Try writing a definition of these words to see if you thoroughly understand what the Bible teaches about the finished work of Christ. It's not that easy. Let's start with *propitiation*. Here are some references in the New Testament where this word is used: Romans 3:25, Hebrews 2:17, 1 John 2:2 and 4:10. The word "propitiation" comes from a word from the Greek (the original language of the New Testament) which basically means "to satisfy wrath by sacrifice." The ancient pagan Greeks used this word when they spoke of appeasing their gods or doing something to obtain the favor of the gods. However, these ideas are not found in the Bible. God is not a bloodthirsty god who needs to be appeased! The idea of placating a vengeful god is totally foreign to Scripture. The Bible teaches that God is love and desires to have fellowship with man. But God is also holy and righteous. Therefore He cannot just smile and sweep sin under the rug and say, "Boys will be boys!" In fact, the Bible teaches that God has wrath and that this wrath is directed against sin (Roman 1:18). And the righteous laws of God in this moral universe which He has created demand that the "penalty of sin is death" (Romans 6:23). Before God's mercy can be extended to man, something must be done to remove the blockade of sin as well as satisfy the righteous claims of God's wrath against sin.

Man, of course, is helpless at this point. The problem cannot become the solution! And there is nothing that man can do by himself to win the favor of God. Here again the pagan idea of doing something religious to gain the favor of the gods is not even hinted at in the New Testament. God already favors man, as John 3:16 clearly states. But the question of God's wrath and judgment against sin must be settled and the barrier of man's sin taken away before the free benefits of salvation can be offered to man. This is precisely where Christ is the propitiation for our sins. Because He sacrificially took and suffered the righteous judgment of God against sin, Christ not only died to take away man's sin, but He thus satisfied or propitiated God's wrath against sin.

Redemption is another aspect of the finished work of Christ. Read the following New Testament Scriptures which have to do with redemption: Galatians 3:13 and 4:5, Ephesians 1:7, 1 Peter 1:18-19. There are several Greek words which are translated, "redeem." In New Testament times these words were used particularly in reference to slavery. Together these words give us the concept of redemption. To redeem means "to buy out of, and remove from, the market in order to set at liberty." In the context of salvation, redemption refers to the work of Christ in setting us free from the bondage and slavery of sin with all its awful connections and consequences.

In redemption, not only have we been bought back and set free from the slave market of sin, but we have been placed as sons in the family of God. This is certainly a step further than emancipation. The word "adoption," by the way, in Galatians 4:5, does not refer to adoption as we know it today, but rather to the Roman adoption ceremony of those days. In this official family action a true son was recognized has having all the rights and privileges and dignity of a son who had come of age. As redeemed sinners, this is our present position in God's family. What grace!

Although we did not pay silver or gold (1 Peter 1:18), we must remember that the cost of our redemption was high. The ransom price was the precious blood of Christ. There is no teaching in the Scriptures that the ransom was paid to Satan, as some have suggested. This notion is pushing the background of the slave market too far. The ransom price was simply what the righteous government of God demanded for our release from the effects of sin (Hebrews 9:22). Have you ever thanked the Lord for the ransom price He was willing to pay out for you?

Reconciliation completes the threefold view of the finished work of Christ. Propitiation, which deals with the wrath of God, is the God-ward aspect of the work. Redemption is concerned with our enslavement and entrapment by sin and is thus the sin-ward aspect of Christ's work. Reconciliation is the man-ward aspect of the finished work of Christ, because it directly relates to our fellowship with God. The word "reconciliation" is used in Romans 5:10, 2 Corinthians 5:18-20, and Colossians 1:20-22. The basic meaning of the word "reconcile," as determined from the Greek language, is "to change completely." In reference to salvation, reconciliation is the act by which God brings man into a completely changed relationship with Himself—from enmity and hostility and alienation to friendship and harmony and fellowship. Notice that reconciliation is a one-way act of God toward man and does not involve the idea of mutual concession between God and man. There is no He-gives-a-little-and-we-give-a-little, as in a marriage reconciliation. Remember that God does not need to change His attitude toward us or meet us halfway. We are the guilty party—unloving, self-willed, and hostile (Colossians 1:21). We, not God, need to be changed completely.

A wonderful illustration of reconciliation is seen in our Lord's story of the lost son in Luke 15:11-32. When the son repents and acknowledges his guilt to the father, he is brought back into a happy and harmonious state of fellowship with the father. He is not just forgiven and allowed back on the property, he is welcomed back into the family with open arms and celebration!

The finished work of Christ is universal in its scope. Look closely at 1 John 2:2, 1 Peter 1:18-19, and 2 Corinthians 5:19, and you will see that Christ's death was sufficient to take care of all the sins of the world— unlimited in its coverage and provision. But that does not mean that everyone has salvation. The finished work of Christ is only efficacious or effectual for those who believe. Think of the GI Bill as an illustration. "Unlimited" government funds were available so that all persons under the Bill could get a college education at government expense. But payments were only effective for those who signed up and went to school. Sufficient and provisional for all, but only effectual for some!

A greater appreciation for the finished work of Christ will result as we come to a fuller understanding of propitiation, redemption, and reconciliation. What blessing for the growing Christian to first realize, and then rest in the finished work of Christ!

33

Coincidence or Providence

Esther 4:14b, NIV   And who knows but that
you have come to royal position for such a
time as this?
Read the entire book of Esther.

Is there such a thing as coincidence in your life
as a growing Christian? Can you just happen to be in
the right place at the right time? And what about the
wrong place at the wrong time? Or does God control
and guide your destiny, even the people you meet and
the places you visit and the particular times involved?
Coincidence—or Providence?

The answer to the question above is both simple
and complex. It is simple because the straightforward,
one-word answer is Providence. The Bible teaches that
God is not only sovereign in controlling all things at
all times, but is actually programming and guiding
events in accordance with His eternal purposes. Ephesians 1:11 says that He "works out everything in conformity with the purpose of His will." (See also Psalm

33:11 and Isaiah 43:13.) Nothing happens by pure chance or accident, and what appears to be merely fortunate or unfortunate circumstance is really the outworking of God's plans. However, the answer to the question of coincidence or Providence is also very complex. That is, it is complex from the human perspective because of our finite limitations. We don't always have the big picture to show us what God is doing and why He is doing it. "For as the heavens are higher than the earth, so are My ways higher than your ways, and My thoughts than your thoughts" (Isaiah 55:9, KJV). How far God allows the sinful will of man, as well as the will of Satan, to operate in this world in specific instances is not easily determined. Again we must acknowledge, "How unsearchable are His judgments and unfathomable His ways!" (Romans 11:33). And how God is able to permit the evil and cruelty that has been perpetrated by men and devils and still "work out everything in conformity with the purpose of His will" is beyond our finite comprehension. When and where God interrupts His natural laws by miraculous, supernatural intervention is not always clear. And what exact relationship exists between a believer's prayers (answered and "unanswered") and the outworking of God's predetermined plans and purposes does not have a simple answer. We do know, however, that "the effective prayer of a righteous man can accomplish much" (James 5:16), and also that "God causes all things to work together for good to those who love God" (Romans 8:28). So while the biblical answer to our original question is Providence and not coincidence or chance in any way, shape, or form, we must acknowledge that our comprehension of this answer is

God's workings in history are sometimes better appreciated than investigated. (Read Psalms 131 and 139.)

An appreciation of Providence is one of the benefits that comes to growing Christians when they read the book of Esther. Providence is the overall theme of this Old Testament book. Although we do not find the name of God mentioned even once in the book of Esther, throughout the book we are conscious of God working things together behind the scenes to accomplish His purposes. It is not coincidence, but Providence that is obviously at work in the events of Esther. The name of God is not seen, but the hand of God is everywhere evident in this book of Scripture. In fact, the concept of Providence is actually enhanced in Esther because God chose not to put His name in the headlines but rather everywhere between the lines. There is a great practical lesson here for us. Many times God does not show Himself in an obvious way in His dealings with us, and yet we can be sure that He is silently and continually at work in our lives to accomplish His good purposes (Philippians 1:6).

The events of the book of Esther took place around 475 B.C. in the land of Persia (where the country of Iran is today). The Jews had been forced to leave their homeland as captives many years before (586 B.C.) when the Babylonian army under Nebuchadnezzar had conquered their nation and burned the temple. After Babylon fell to the Persians in 539 B.C., the Persian king, Cyrus, issued an edict which granted permission to the Jews to return to the land of Judah. About fifty thousand Jews returned to Jerusalem at that time, but many others chose to remain in the vicinity of Babylon and other areas of the expanding Persian empire. Some of the Jews prospered under Persian rule, and a few even held political office. Daniel and Nehemiah, for example, held high positions in the Persian government. (See Daniel 6 and Nehemiah 1.) Esther's older cousin and guardian, Mordecai, also held some kind of government post. The phrase "sitting at the king's gate" in Esther 2:21 seems to indicate this. However, there was also a significant amount of anti-Semitism at this time, as Esther 3:13 and 9:1 indicate. It was in this historical setting that Haman, a high government official and the villain of the story, was confident that his scheme to kill all the Jews of the empire would be carried out (3:8,13). Naturally speaking, it looked like all hope for the Jews was gone. The die was literally cast (3:7). The design of Satan to do away with God's people, from whom the predicted Messiah would come, seemed foolproof. But Providence was at work.

Xerxes I (Ahasuerus is the Hebrew form of this name) was more than a little miffed when Queen Vashti refused to show off her beautiful body at the king's banquet and drinking party (Esther 1:10-12). Vashti's exile opened the door for a new queen to attain this influential position with King Ahasuerus. Providence! And it just worked out that beautiful Esther happened to be at the right place at the right time and was selected as the new queen. More Providence! Let's pause for a practical lesson. Is it not possible that God has sovereignly ordained your good looks or unique abilities to use in a special way for His glory? Think of all the factors that "just happened" to fall into place for Esther. Even the king's mood happened to be just right on Esther's date of appearance. This is especially significant when we learn from extra-biblical sources that Xerxes I was a very cruel, moody, and temperamental emperor. This fact is helpful in understanding verses like Esther 4:11. So here again we see Providence at work in bringing Esther to the place and position in God's plan and purpose to save His people. It should be noted that God in no way placed Esther in a compromising situation. Her night with the king (2:14-16) was not an act of fornication. All the women in the king's harem were considered married to the king. Xerxes I was a polygamist, but Esther was not an adulteress. Perhaps Esther 4:14b could apply directly to the position or job that God has placed you in right now. Never think in terms of coincidence or chance or accident, but rather Providence.

Meanwhile, Mordecai just happened to overhear a plot to assassinate King Ahasuerus. This information was passed on to the king through Esther and it was documented in the royal chronicles (Esther 2:21-23). It wasn't long before these events also proved to be providential. It just so happened that one night King Ahasuerus could not sleep. He decided to pass the time by reading the royal records. And sure enough, he read about Mordecai's loyalty and decided to reward him (6:1-3). God was even in control of the king's insomnia and the reading material he selected. Now about this time wicked Haman arrived at the palace in order to request permission to hang Mordecai. Haman hated this faithful Jew because he refused to bow down to any mere man, even the exalted Haman. The king asked Haman, "What is to be done for the man whom the king desires to honor?" (6:6). Haman's eyes lit up as he thought of ways he himself could be paraded around town with royal robes and crown. Little did he dream that the king had Mordecai in mind. And guess who had to lead the parade for Mordecai? What Providence!

Esther had come to the conclusion that she must act on behalf of her people even if it cost her life. Just because Esther was providentially brought to her influential position did not mean that life would be easy or that God would not test her faith. God tests our faith! (See James 1:3 and 1 Peter 1:7.) Are you being severely tested right now in the position where God had placed you? Can you by faith say, as Esther said, "If I perish, I perish" (Esther 4:16)? It certainly wasn't coincidence that Ahasuerus not only extended the golden scepter to Esther (5:2) but offered her up to half of the Persian empire as well (5:3). This was almost unbelievable! Esther was hoping only that the king would give her an opportunity to plead for mercy for her people. Providence! God is still able to do "exceeding abundantly beyond all that we ask or think" (Ephesians 3:20). Incidentially, what would you have asked for if half the Persian empire had been offered to you?

As a result of Esther's courage and faithfulness, wicked Haman was eliminated and the Jewish people were saved. Of course, from the divine perspective it was Providence all the way. Even Haman's cast of the dice (Esther 3:7) was controlled by the hand of God so that the Jews would have eight months to prepare for their defense (Proverbs 16:33). The fact that the Persian edict to kill all the Jews could not be revoked (Esther 8:8) was also part of God's plan. The new decree which countered this "law of the Medes and Persians" not only resulted in the preservation of the Jews, but the elimination of many anti-Semites. The feast of Purim, which is still observed annually by many Jewish people, originated as a celebration of these events.

All these events were the result of Providence, not coincidence. Events in our lives today are not governed by coincidence or chance. They are all part of God's providential plan for our ultimate blessing.

34

Without Excuse

Romans 1:20   For since the creation of the
world His invisible attributes, His eternal
power and divine nature, have been clearly
seen, being understood through what has
been made, so that they are without excuse.

"If you can show me conclusive evidence that
God exists, than I will immediately become a Christian!" Have you ever had unbelievers say that to you?
They presuppose, of course, that you cannot show
them any concrete evidence for the existence of God.
They truly believe that no such objective evidence exists—that it is only your highly subjective and suspect
faith that has created God in your simple mind. "You
may be a very sincere person," they say, "but unfortunately you have been brainwashed by your religion.
Your life of faith may be very meaningful to you, but
in reality you are very naive and have simply been
duped by your unsophisticated family or friends." Yes,
those unbelievers are convinced that there is not a

scrap of evidence to support your "erroneous" belief in God.

Is there any solid proof for God's existence? Is there any objective evidence that we Christians can point out to unbelievers in order to show conclusively that God exists? According to the Bible, God has given mankind sufficient evidence of Himself so that no blind leap of faith is necessary. In fact, Romans 1:20 states that the evidence for the existence of God is so overwhelming and clear that an individual has no excuse for not believing in God. And Romans 1:20 is not just talking about people who have been exposed to the Bible or Christianity. It includes all persons from the beginning of time. The Bible says emphatically that any person who turns away from the evidence and denies the existence of God is a fool. (See Psalm 14 and Psalm 53, and note the universal context in verse 2 of these psalms.)

Well then, where is this indisputable evidence for the existence of God? It is all around us in nature. Romans 1:20 indicates that God's existence and divine nature are "understood through what has been made." The natural world all about us cries out for an explanation of its existence, and the only adequate explanation is God. Not everyone has been exposed to the special revelation which God has given of Himself in the Scriptures and in the person of Jesus Christ, but all of mankind has been given the general revelation of God in nature. The proof of God which the skeptic so smugly demands is staring him in the face every day.

Theologians categorize the evidence which we find in nature as the naturalistic arguments for the existence of God. Three of the naturalistic arguments are known as the cosmological, the teleological, and the anthropoligical arguments. You might think that these arguments are highly complex and complicated because of their long and technical-sounding names. However, they are really quite simple and easy to follow once the basic causal argument is understood.

The causal argument consists of two statements, or laws, and a conclusion. The first law of the causal argument states that "for every effect there must be a cause." That is, there must be a cause behind every single thing that happens. A car moving down the street, for example, did not just materialize out of thin air and start driving itself. There are causes behind the effect of the moving car. The second law of the causal argument states that "no effect can be greater (quantitatively or qualitatively) than its cause." That is, a cause must always be equal to, or greater than, the effect it causes. A large tree falling over, for example, must have a cause behind that fall which is quantitatively greater than a light summer breeze. A beautiful painting must be caused by something qualitatively greater than a few cans of paint falling on a canvas. Now behind every immediate cause there is obviously a chain of prior causes. Behind a printed page, for example, is an immediate printing press "cause." But what caused the printing press, and what caused the cause of the printing press, etc., etc.? It is not difficult to see that the logical conclusion of the causal argument is that behind everything there is either an infinite and eternal chain of greater and greater causes, or there is ultimately a first great Cause which is itself infinite and eternally uncaused. And when you really think about it, there is not too much difference between these two options! The Christian takes a reasonable step (not a blind leap!) of faith at this point and believes that the God of the Bible is this infinite and eternal First Cause. Unbelievers ridicule Christians for this step of faith by asking, "What caused God?" They think that this question somehow wins their case or gets them off the hook, but they are actually showing their own ignorance of logic. Every rational person, including unbelievers, must logically conclude on the basis of the causal argument that somewhere at the beginning of the line there has got to be an uncaused cause. The unbeliever who labels this uncaused cause "Big Bang" or "Eternal Universe" takes just as much of a leap of faith as the Christian who believes in God. We could reasonably ask at this point, "Who has really been brainwashed in their thinking?"

Now when the causal argument is applied to the matter and motion of the universe, it becomes the cosmological argument for the existence of God. When applied to the design and order found throughout the universe, it becomes the teleological argument. And when applied to the immaterial aspects of man such as his rational, moral, and aesthetic nature, it becomes the anthropological argument. Let's trace each of these naturalistic arguments for the existence of God in a little more detail.

The matter of the universe is an effect. There must be an adequate cause for all the stars and planets as well as every single atom and subatomic particle that exists. The causal argument demands a first cause or Prime Maker for the material of this universe. The motion of this universe is also an effect. The causal argument indicates that there must be a first cause for all the intricate movements in this universe. Everything from orbiting electrons to reverse spinning moons to spiraling galaxies must be accounted for! A Prime Mover is called for by the causal argument to explain the complex motion of the universe. The cosmological argument cannot be denied. The only adequate rational answer to the matter and motion of the universe is the answer of Romans 1:20: His eternal power.

What about the teleological argument? We don't have to look far to realize that there is plenty of design within our universe. Consider things like the structure of the atom or the marvel of the human eye. Consider the delicate balance of nature here on earth. Consider the many natural laws which govern the vast universe. Did all of these effects come about by pure chance? The causal argument demands that each of these effects must have a greater cause. Order and design and structure and law demand an intelligent cause. It seems so obvious! (See Psalm 94:9.) No wonder Romans 1:20 uses the words "clearly seen." How can any sophisticated theory of evolution adquately explain the how and why of the origin of these effects? Have you ever watched a spider spin a web? Is it even conceivable that this highly complex creature with its web machine and web know-how could have come about through random mutations? Think of the human brain. What principle of evolution can explain the development of such a complex computer, the capacity of which is never fully utilized by any individual? Surely the wisdom of a Creator is stamped all over this universe.

In the anthropological argument the many different nonmaterial aspects of mankind are considered as effects, and then the causal argument is applied. The fact that human beings are rational, have a moral nature, and can perceive beauty and harmony means that the cause of these effects must also be rational, moral, and aesthetic. The fact that humans have a will and personality means that their cause must be volitional and personal. Romans 1:20 declares that not only God's power but also His nature must be seen in what He has made. It's easy to see that as the many different immaterial effects of man are examined, the first cause becomes more and more a description of the nature of the God of the Bible. To say that all these effects in mankind have come into being without God is to deny the causal argument and to opt for the idea that they all came about through a change-guided rearrangement of molecular matter. Does anyone have an acceptable excuse for believing such a myth?

The naturalistic arguments which God has made intrinsic to His work of creation are so obvious that His Word of revelation declares that unbelievers are without excuse forever! How much better to go with the evidence now and agree with the psalmist: "The heavens declare the glory of God; the skies proclaim the work of His hands" (Psalm 19:1, NIV). "I will praise You because I am fearfully and wonderfully made; Your works are wonderful, I know that full well" (Psalm 139:14).

35

From Rags to Riches

*Ruth 1:16,*NIV   But Ruth replied, "Don't urge me to leave you or to turn back from you. Where you go I will go, and where you stay I will stay. Your people will be my people and your God my God.
Read the entire book of Ruth.

A Cinderella story is always interesting and intriguing. The story is even more fascinating and attractive if we know that it's true. Most exciting of all is when the story comes right out of Scripture. Here the story is not only true, but it is told to us by God Himself. The book of Ruth in the Bible is an exciting rags-to-riches story. As we read this wonderful narrative let us visualize ourselves as God's children sitting at the feet of our heavenly Father and listening to Him tell the story to us.

The story of Ruth takes place during the period of the judges in Israel's history. Spiritual and moral conditions were not the greatest at this time. The nation of Israel had backslidden considerably since the days of the great leadership of Moses and Joshua, and now only periodically was a judge raised up by God to stem the downward spiral. We read that during the days of the judges "everyone did what was right in their own eyes" (Judges 17:6 and 21:25). It is against this dark background that the beautiful story of Ruth stands out in marked contrast—especially the main characters, Boaz and Ruth.

The focus of Ruth 1 is the life-changing *decision* of Ruth. Ruth was from Moab—a Gentile and an outsider to God's covenant blessings upon Israel. Ruth had married into a poor, Hebrew family which had migrated to Moab. But her husband had died and she had no children. Ruth was certainly experiencing the worst possible situation for that time and culture: poor, bereaved, and childless. When her widowed mother-in-law, Naomi, decided to return to Judah, Ruth was confronted with a major, life-changing decision. Should she stay with her own people in her own country or burn her bridges behind her and go with Naomi to Israel? Ruth decided wholeheartedly to go to Israel. The text above is Ruth's classic and inspiring statement of commitment at the time of her decision. Naturally speaking, it was much more logical for Ruth to stay in Moab. Opportunities for remarriage and family and security were far greater there. For a Gentile girl to go to Judah with a poor old widow like Naomi held nothing but a rags-to-rags prospect. But Ruth was *determined* (verse 18) to go against all these odds. Why? Because Ruth had come to put her trust in the God of Israel. Ruth loved Naomi, and she must have loved her own people as well, but it was the God of Naomi that made the difference (verse 16). Ruth was confident that the Lord, in whom she had come to trust, would take care of her future.

The Lord calls us to make significant decisions, too. The choice to follow Christ, for example, is most important and may have been quite costly for some of us. To be estranged from family and ostracized by friends for the sake of Christ is not the greatest feeling in the world. How much easier to be like Orpah in the story. Orpah was in the same situation as Ruth (Ruth 1:4-5). Orpah started in the right direction (verses 6-7). She was emotionally moved about the decision (verses 9,14), and said she was going to go all the way (verse 10). But Orpah didn't. She went back to her people and country and gods (verse 15). How true of many would-be followers of Christ today. The Lord also calls growing Christians to make Ruth-like decisions. Choosing a life of service for the Lord may result in having very little earthly wealth or security. To say yes to God's call to the foreign mission field may involve leaving family and friends. As in the case of Ruth, only the Lord Himself can give us the confidence and courage and faith that we need for making this kind of decision.

In chapter 2 we see the *dedication* of Ruth. That is, we see her dedication to the decision she had made to follow Naomi and to seek refuge under the wings of the Lord, the God of Israel (verse 12). As soon as Ruth arrived in Bethlehem, she went out to the fields and gleaned for herself and Naomi. Ruth had come to know that the God of Israel had graciously incorporated the gleaning clause into His law as a means of provision for poor people. Any person in need could always go into any field and harvest the leftovers. (See Leviticus 19:9-10 and Deuteronomy 24:19-21.) Gleaning was long and arduous toil, but Ruth never complained or wavered in the commitment she had made. Would we have been so dedicated? Many Christians have looked and sounded very dedicated at altar calls for Christian service, but before long the labor in the fields determines those who are truly committed.

To fully appreciate the spiritual lessons to be found in Ruth's dedication, the place of Boaz in the story needs to be understood. Boaz was not only the wealthy landowner and prince of this Cinderella story, he was a kinsman-redeemer. Just what this unique position involved will be explained shortly, but in summary it can be said that Boaz is a beautiful picture or illustration of the Lord Jesus Christ, who is our Kinsman-Redeemer. Thus the fields of Boaz where Ruth labored can represent the field of the Lord in this picture God has painted for us. To glean in the field of the Lord is to be occupied with the interests of God and separated from the fields of the world. As Boaz told Ruth not to glean in another field (Ruth 2:8), so our Lord tells us not to be drawn away by the temporal values and snares of this world (2 Corinthians 6:17; 2 Timothy 2:4; 1 John 2:15). As Boaz promised Ruth provision and protection in his field (Ruth 2:9), so our Lord promises to provide for us and protect us if we stay in His field (Hebrews 13:5-6). As Boaz served Ruth the fruit of his field which completely satisfied her (Ruth 2:14), so our Lord ministers His Word to us, the food that alone can fully satisfy our souls (Jeremiah 15:16). As Boaz sweetened the rewards of Ruth's labor in his field (Ruth 2:15-16), so our Lord richly rewards our active occupation with the interests of God (Matthew 6:33; 11:28-29; Luke 6:38). May we not only learn and appreciate these lessons of the field, but let us be dedicated gleaners and experience all these blessings from the Lord of the harvest.

In the last two chapters of the book our attention is drawn more and more to the *devotion* of Ruth to Boaz. It doesn't take much reading between the lines to realize that by the end of chapter 2, Ruth and Boaz are falling in love and that the devotion of Ruth is really a response to the love and kindness of Boaz. The actions of Ruth and Naomi in chapter 3 may appear at first to be a little strange and even questionable, but some background knowledge of the role of the kinsman-redeemer should clear up any misunderstanding. Certain stipulations of God's law were designed to care for extended family and kin. According to Leviticus 25:25, when an individual became so poor that he had to sell or forfeit his property, a prosperous relative was to redeem or buy back the property for the poor family member. The Hebrew word that is used for this close realtive is "goel" and is translated either as "redeem" or "relative" in the Old Testament. This person is thus called a kinsman-redeemer. Another responsibility of a close relative is found in Deuteronomy 25:5-10. If a husband died before having a male heir, then an unmarried brother of the deceased was to marry the widow and produce the firstborn son in his brother's name. If there were no eligible brothers available, then the duty passed to the closest eligible male relative. In Ruth's case there were no brothers available, and thus Boaz, as a close relative, had a responsibility toward Ruth as well as toward the family property which Naomi was forced to sell out of poverty. So Ruth's behavior in chapter 3 was not some indiscreet escapade, but rather her legally proper initiative to tell Boaz that she was willing for him to take on his responsibilities as kinsman-redeemer (verse 9). Naomi knew that after the harvest party, Boaz, along with his servants, would be spending the night at the threshing floor in order to guard the winnowed grain. (See Judges 6:11.) Naomi's plan was just a sensible and logical (and also romantic!) way for Ruth to communicate her wishes to Boaz.

The honorable behavior of Boaz in response to the devotion of Ruth, as well as his noble actions toward the other close relative in chapter 4 point up the excellent character of Boaz and remind us again of our own Kinsman-Redeemer, the Lord Jesus. As the wealthy Boaz willingly bought back the lost property and married Ruth, the poor Gentile foreigner, so Christ in His love has recovered all our "lost property" and taken us poor "foreigners" to be His bride (Ephesians 2:12-13; 5:31-32). There were three prerequisites necessary for the kinsman-redeemer: he had to be a close relative, wealthy, and willing. As our Kinsman-Redeemer, the Lord Jesus fulfills all three prerequisites perfectly. Is He a close relative? Hebrews 2:5-16 makes clear that the eternal Son of God took on humanity precisely so that He could become our Kinsman in order to redeem us. Is He a wealthy close relative? 1 Peter 1:18-19 emphasizes that only Jesus Christ has the means to pay the infinite price of redemption: a perfect life. Is He a wealthy and willing close relative? Mark 10:45 tells us that the Son of Man gave His life as a sacrifice in order to redeem us. What is our response?

Like all Cinderella stories, the book of Ruth has a happy ending. The rags-to-riches aspect is emphasized at the end of chapter 4 where we learn that Ruth was

the great-grandmother of King David. And when we
realize that this poor woman from Moab is thus
brought into the messianic line (Matthew 1:5), we are
further amazed at the riches of God's grace—grace
that is still available to take sinners from rags to
riches.

36

Lost Forever

Luke 16:26   And besides all this, between us and you there is a great [gulf] fixed, in order that those who wish to come over from here to you may not be able, and that none may cross over from there to us.
Read Luke 16:19-31.

Forever is a word which cannot be fully visualized. Try it. It's like thinking about halfway to infinity. Now think about the idea of existing forever—and ever and ever and ever and ever and ever and ever and ever. . . . What if such an idea were true? The Bible teaches us that we will exist forever. What started out as a simple mental exercise now becomes an emotional experience. As the concept of existing forever grows on us, our emotions may range from joy to fear, depending on our relationship with God. The Bible teaches that believers will exist forever with God in a place called heaven, while unbelievers will exist forever without God in a place called hell.

Hell is not a pleasant subject to think about and most unbelievers simply dismiss it from their minds, except for using it as an occasional curse word. Some unbelievers, however, would agree that there ought to be some kind of hell. After all, if the Stalins and the Hitlers of this world can get away from their crimes and atrocities by merely dying, which is common to all of mankind anyway, then life is totally unfair and unjust. Somewhere along the line it all has to come out in the wash with some kind of standard upheld and penalty meted out, or else any talk about human decency and dignity and rights and good causes is just a joke. Although many people will go along with this line of reasoning to a point, they do not want to accept the biblical concept of hell. Why? Becuase the Bible teaches that hell is not just for Hitler and Stalin, but for every unbeliever. All have sinned and fallen short of God's standards (Romans 3:23).

In the account of the rich man and Lazarus in Luke 16, the Bible gives us some important teaching concerning hell. The word "hell" in verse 23 is transliterated "hades" in some versions. Technically speaking, hades is a description of the present situation of deceased unbelievers awaiting their final consignment to hell. Since the Lord Jesus was relating what appears to be a true story and not just a parable, it is not surprising that He used the word hades to describe the condition of the rich man, because the final day of judgment for the damned had obviously not yet taken place. The description of hades here in Luke 16 is certainly applicable to hell: the place of those who are lost forever.

In verses 19-21 we read that hell is a place of surprising reversal. In this life the rich man was successful, while Lazarus had nothing. The Pharisees who were listening to this story (verse 14) would have understood the rich man to be someone who was apparently blessed most favorably by God. And poor suffering Lazarus would be understood to be an individual who was under the discipline of God. After all, he appeared to be forsaken by God and left to be licked by street dogs, which made him ceremonially unclean. But after death, Lazarus, of all people, was found secure in Abraham's bosom. This phrase would be understood by Christ's audience as a description of eternal bliss in paradise. What a surprising reversal!

Notice that the rich man is not said to be a Scrooge or a Simon Legree. In fact, verse 21 may indicate that he permitted Lazarus to have the leftovers from his table. This rich man would be typical of a lot of Americans today—apparently enjoying God's favor and by no means deliberately neglecting the poor and suffering. Even token efforts of concern are characteristic of most citizens. Certainly God would not send a "good" person like this to hell! But the Lord Jesus corrects such wrong thinking with this story. The Bible is not teaching here that all rich people go to hell and all poor people go the heaven. Luke 16 does not even tell us why this rich man went to hell and Lazarus went to heaven, although the rich man's self-centeredness may be a hint. The actual means of salvation, namely Christ, is given to us in many other Scriptures but is not the focus of this story. This Scripture emphasizes that status and position in this life may be surprisingly reversed in the life to come. We Christians must share this truth with our status conscious society.

In verses 23-24 we find that *hell is a place of painful*

retribution. Some unbelievers have the idea that hell will be some kind of pleasant reunion with all their old friends. The Bible does not even suggest such a thought. The rich man was suffering torment (verse 23) and agony (verse 24) and did not even want anyone to join him in such a horrible place (verse 28). There was no relief, not even the slightest ray of hope. Many people ask: Is such punishment fair? It is not so much a question of fairness but of choice. Suppose I'm drowning and I choose not to believe it, and I choose not to take the life preserver which is thrown to me. Are the consequences fair? Unbelievers choose to go to hell because they either refuse to believe the truth or they refuse to do something about it. In Matthew 13:42, the Lord spoke of hell as a place where there will be "weeping and gnashing of teeth." Because they chose to go to hell instead of heaven, some unbelievers will weep with unending regret and some will gnash their teeth in bitter anger against God forever. If you are reading these lines and you are not a Christian, fortunately it is still not too late for you to avoid the painful retribution of hell. Choose to commit your life to Christ now before you are lost forever.

Luke 16:25 teaches that *hell is a place of conscious remembrance.* Hell is not cessation of awareness or memory. The rich man was not only aware of what he was missing as he viewed Lazarus, but he was able to vividly recall his past. In fact, he is commanded to think back on his lifetime on earth. (The imperative is used for "remember" in verse 25.) We are fortunate in this life to be able to blot out, at least partially, bad memories of past mistakes. This human characteristic tends to make life more pleasant. But in hell there will be no such convenience. Every guilty conscience will be fully awake and active. Probably the Lord Jesus had this gnawing conscience in mind when He described hell as a place "where their worm does not die" (Mark 9:44-48). What could be worse than remembering forever the missed opportunities to believe the simple truth?

We are taught that *hell is a place of no return* in verse 26 of Luke 16. There is no second chance in hell. Any idea of reincarnation is utterly foreign to Scripture. "It is appointed for men to die once, and after this comes judgment" (Hebrews 9:27). And hell is not a place of temporary punishment with eventual admittance to heaven after a period of purification. The Bible definitely does not teach that everyone is going to make it to heaven in the end. (See Matthew 25:41, 46.) The fact that there is a great gulf fixed means that hell is a permanent situation. Luke 16:26 makes clear that even if someone in heaven wanted to help someone in hell, this is an impossiblity. Mercy is for this life only. The only good news here is that the fixed boundary means that believers are eternally secure in heaven. Believers can no more fall from heaven than Christ can fall from heaven, because the blessed position of every Christian is in Christ forever.

Finally, in verses 27-31, we see that *hell is a place of awful realization.* The rich man was forced to realize that to reject or neglect the truth of the Scriptures meant to be lost forever. Like his five brothers on earth, the rich man had access to "Moses and the Prophets" during his lifetime (verse 29). This a reference to the Old Testament Scriptures, of course. Remember that the New Testament hadn't been written yet. For anyone who was open to the truth, the Bible was sufficient evidence—and it still is! Miracles will not convince the hardened skeptic in spite of what the rich man thought and argued (verse 30). As the old saying goes, "A man convinced against his will, is of the same opinion still."

Proof of the declaration in verse 31 took place not too long after our Lord told this story. A man named Lazarus (of all names!) was raised from the dead and came back to witness to the truth of Christ and the Scriptures. (See John 11.) The Pharisees who would not listen to "Moses and the Prophets" were not persuaded to become believers even though someone had been raised from the dead. These stubborn and calloused unbelievers plotted instead to kill Jesus (John 11:53), and Lazarus as well (John 12:10). Our Lord's own resurrection soon after did not change their unbelief either. How awful for those unbelievers, along with the rich man and any other rejecters of Scripture, then and now, to realize after death that they are lost forever.

It is significant that the Lord Jesus spoke more of hell than of heaven, according to what is recorded in the four Gospels. Why would our loving Lord, who always went about doing good, spend so much time talking about such an unpleasant subject? 2 Peter 3:9 gives the simple answer: Our God does not want anyone to be lost forever in hell.

37

Song and Sacrifice

2 Chronicles 29:27-28 Then Hezekiah gave
the order to offer the burnt offering on the
altar. When the burnt offering began,
the song to the LORD also began with the
trumpets, accompanied by the instruments
of David, king of Israel. While the whole
assembly worshiped, the singers also sang and
the trumpets sounded; all this continued until
the burnt offering was finished.
Read 2 Chronicles 29–31.

King Hezekiah of Judah is no stranger to students of ancient history. His name and military activities are well-documented in the Assyrian records of
King Sennacherib. These inscriptions on clay prisms
date from the seventh century B.C. and support and
corroborate the inspired record of King Hezekiah's activities as given in 2 Kings and 2 Chronicles. The rock
hewn water tunnel which Hezekiah constructed underneath the city of Jerusalem (2 Kings 20:20; 2
Chronicles 32:30) is documented in the Siloam in-

scription which was inscribed on the wall of the tunnel itself. This underground passageway is well-known to Holy Land visitors today and still carries water from the Gihon Spring to the Pool of Siloam. But Hezekiah's important spiritual activities are known to us only from the Bible. Hezekiah was one of the good kings of Judah, and there are a number of spiritual principles that emerge from the biblical account of his life. Students of history may learn quite a bit about King Hezekiah from the secular records, but growing Christians can come to know and appreciate the divine lessons from Hezekiah's life that God has incorporated into the scriptural record.

King Hezekiah's father was wicked King Ahaz. This evil king had shut down the temple (2 Chronicles 28:24) and even stooped to the idolatrous practice of burning his sons in pagan sacrifice (verse 3). But when Hezekiah came to the throne, "he did right in the sight of the Lord" (2 Chronicles 29:2). The first thing he did was reopen the doors of the temple (verse 3), cleanse the holy place (verse 5), and reestablish the public worship of the Lord (verse 35). A great revival began and swept through Judah. This revival is the subject of 2 Chronicles 29–31.

As you read through the record of Hezekiah's revival, think of revival today—in your own soul or in the life of your church or fellowship group. In this framework you will see some divine principles for revival begin to emerge from the text. For example, all of King Hezekiah's activities in repairing and cleansing the temple in chapter 29 certainly have their spiritual counterparts today. Remember that Christians are now the temples of the Holy Spirit both as individuals (1 Corinthians 6:19) and collectively as the church

(1 Corinthians 3:16). If we want revival, we must be prepared to remove unholy things from our temples. What unholy thoughts or habits need to be removed from the temple of your body and life for revival to begin? What practices or traditions need to be corrected in your fellowship in order for revival to sweep through your church? Many other principles for revival are scattered throughout these chapters. Principles such as obedience to the laws of God (2 Chronicles 30:16), renewed giving (2 Chronicles 31:4), and total commitment in service (verse 21) are all significant and necessary ingredients for true revival.

Another important principle of revival, or a principle for just plain Christian living, comes out of our text above. In these verses (2 Chronicles 29:27-28) we see that singing accompanied the burnt offering. Song and sacrifice went together. When the sacrifice began, the song to the Lord also began (verse 27) and continued until the sacrifice was completed (verse 28). It was God's intention that the singing and the offering take place together. Let's call this "the divine principle of song and sacrifice." "Song" to the Lord is an expression of joy and thanksgiving. It's hard to sing praises with the mouth without joy in the heart. "Sacrifice" involves a solemn recognition of the seriousness of sin and the payment for sin. As the Old Testament believers viewed the burning flesh of the sacrifice they were solemnly reminded of the gravity of their sin and the cost of maintaining a relationship with God. Believers today who understand and practice the principle of sacrifice will invariably be sincere, solemn, and serious about a holy walk before the Lord.

Both song and sacrifice should characterize every growing Christian. They go together. There should be an unmistakable joy as well as a sobering solemnity marking every believer. Unfortunately some Christians go to one unbalanced extreme or the other and consequently distort the gospel, especially when they try to "correct" their fellow believers. Christians who go around looking morbid and gloomy with no smile and no expression of joy convey a distorted concept of Christianity. These Christians may be very earnest and understand the solemnity of the faith, but they need more of the principle of song in their everyday living. After all, they have been saved and their sins are forgiven and they're on their way to heaven. On the other hand, Christians who constantly run around shouting "Praise the Lord!" and "Hallelujah!" in any and all situations misrepresent the good news as well. These Christians may be very genuine and greatly appreciate the joy that only Christ can give, but they need to remember the truth of sacrifice as well as song. There must be that sober and solemn reflection and meditation (even with weeping) concerning the awful price of our redemption, as well as our obligations as redeemed slaves. (See 1 Peter 1:17-19.) The principle of song and sacrifice means that both joy and solemnity are vital aspects of Christian living. They are not mutually exclusive; they should be kept in balance in every believer's life. They should be kept in balance in the worship at church as well. Congregational worship that lacks the joy of celebration and appears to be a funeral service is worship without song. But worship that is only a happy, self-centered, emotional experience, forgetting that the focus and theme of worship is the Lord who created us and loved us and gave Himself for us, is irreverent worship without sacrifice. Do you practice the divine principle of song and sacrifice in your individual and corporate worship? (See 1 Peter 2:4-10 and particularly note verses 5 and 9.)

Particularly emphasized in 2 Chronicles 29:25 is the divine principle of song and sacrifice. Here we see that the combination of singing with the presentation of the burnt offering was not an innovation of King Hezekiah. This order was brought about years before by King David according to a commandment from the Lord. We read about David's organization of the musicians in 1 Chronicles 25 as part of the plans for the temple which was to be built by his son, King Solomon. 1 Chronicles 28:11-21 emphasizes that all these plans for the new temple, both building and service, were given to David by direct revelation from the Lord. It is significant that God wanted singing in connection with the temple worship, because singing had not been part of the tabernacle worship during the wilderness journey from Egypt to Canaan. Song with sacrifice was not commanded in the law of Moses. To sing while animals were being slaughtered and burned upon the altar would be most unusual, especially when the somber implications of the sacrifices were realized. But God wanted singing in connection with the temple worship. Why?

There may be a number of reasons why God waited until the temple was built to bring in singing—reasons that we cannot fully comprehend now. Remember that God's thoughts and ways are higher than our thoughts and ways (Isaiah 55:8-9). One possible reason is that singing could not characterize wilderness worship because God's people were being disciplined in the wilderness for their sins of discontent and unbelief. There they wandered for forty years, apart from God's will, with no song. The Hebrews could no more sing the Lord's song in the wilderness than they could sing the Lord's song in captivity in Babylon years later (Psalm 137:4). After the crossing of the Red Sea and the song of Moses in Exodus 15, there is no singing to the Lord in the inspired record until Numbers 21:17, which is at the end of the forty years of wilderness wandering. What a joyful relief it is to see the Israelites moving forward once again—in the will of God and ready to enter the land of promise. It seems that God's intentions were to formally bring singing into the worship as soon as the land of blessing was fully conquered and occupied and the central sanctuary was established at Jerusalem, the city of God's sovereign choice (Deuteronomy 12:1-14; Psalm 132:13-18). Complete conquering and occupation of the Holy Land did not take place under Joshua or the judges. It remained for King David to capture Jerusalem and bring the ark of the covenant up to God's chosen city (1 Chronicles 15). And then, at the direction of the Lord, David drew up the plans for the temple and the worship to be connected with this final resting place of the ark: the worship of sacrifice with song.

What is the lesson in all of this for the growing Christian? The worship of song and sacrifice is not possible in the wilderness but only in the land of blessing. The proper balance of joy and solemnity is never characteristic of a Christian who is wandering off the path of a close walk with the Lord. A Christian who is being disciplined by the Lord cannot really sing praises to God from the heart; and neither can a wilderness Christian be really serious and earnest in worship. In fact, if the wanderer attempts solemn reflection and worship without repentance, that worship is nothing but a hypocritical front. Only the growing Christian can truly experience the worship of song and sacrifice.

38

Mind Control

Romans 12:2   Be transformed by the
renewing of your mind.
2 Corinthians 10:5, NIV   We take captive
every thought to make it obedient to Christ.
Philippians 2:3   With humility of mind let
each of you regard one another as more
important than himself.
Philippians 4:8, NIV   If anything is excellent
or praiseworthy—think about such things.
1 Peter 1:13   Gird your minds for action.

The title, "Mind Control," is not meant to convey some idea of hypnotic trances or Communist
brainwashings. It has to do with the responsibility of
all growing Christians to control their thinking. The
Bible indicates that our thought life is an extremely
important and vital aspect of being a Christian. What
we are is determined largely by what and how we
think. Proverbs 23:7 says, "As [a person] thinks within
himself, so he is." Scripture not only gives us the responsibility of mind control, it also gives us some def-

inite guidelines to follow in order to have a thought life that is controlled and pleasing to God. Let us look at a few of the many biblical passages dealing with mind control.

In Romans 12:2 we are exhorted to *change perspectives*. We are not to be conformed to this world's way of thinking, but to be transformed to God's way of thinking. Understand that "the world" is not just a label for trash or a list of taboos. The world is basically a system of values which is contrary to the biblical set of values. Our thought patterns must be brought under the control of the divine value system. For example, the world says that if you want to be great, then get to the top, go for it, be number one! But God says that if you want to be truly great then "serve one another" (Matthew 20:25-28). Are we conformed to the world's system of values or transformed to God's set of values? Do we serve one another or manipulate one another? What is our real motive for wanting a leadership position? We can see how easy it is for Christians to operate on the basis of worldly standards rather than biblical standards. We may be not have a problem with drinking or drugs, but we are still worldly if we are trying to be great by some means other than serving one another! This is just one example which points up how different the world's value system is from God's value system. Look at some other biblical values, such as Matthew 6:32-33 and Luke 6:38, and see how different they are from the value system of the world. Growing Christians must constantly evaluate their motives and judgments, because Satan is a master at deceiving the naive into thinking that the two value systems are not all that different.

Romans 12:2 also tells us that the continual renewing of our minds is the only way for our thinking to be transformed from conformity to the world's value system. Renewal of our thinking involves a steady diet of feeding on the Word of God. The constant consumption of biblical standards will renew and control our minds. Our thinking, and thus our actions, will no longer be conformed and controlled by the values of the world but will line up more and more with the value and will of God: "good and acceptable and perfect."

Another principle of mind control is to *capture preoccupations.* In 2 Corinthians 10:5 we see that we are to make every thought an obedient captive to Christ. Immoral thoughts and selfish thoughts must be brought under control just like enemy captives in time of war. Notice that spiritual warfare is the context of this Scripture (verses 3-5). It is almost impossible for us to keep sinful thoughts from flitting through our minds, but we can prevent ourselves from being preoccupied with such thoughts. As Martin Luther said many years ago, "You cannot keep the birds from flying over your head, but you can keep them from building nests in your hair." We can stop fantasizing. We can stop reading certain paperbacks. We can stop watching the kind of movies that will pollute our minds—and maybe certain TV shows, too. In short, we can prevent our minds from becoming preoccupied with thoughts which are not honoring to the Lord Jesus. We can control a lot of what goes into our minds, and we can certainly control the preoccupations of our minds. Let us not allow any harmful thoughts to begin to take control of our thought life.

A humble mind is also an important part of mind control. Although the responsibility to *check pride* is far more easily talked about than practiced, Philippians 2:2-4 gives us some definite guidelines on how to attain humility of mind. Verse 3 gives us some very practical advice on how to start the pride-checking process. Never think of yourself as better or greater than the person you're dealing with, even if you're smarter or richer or more attractive or more athletic. In fact, always consider the other person as more important than yourself. Although God created all men equal, God still tells us in this Scripture that the key to mind control in the area of pride is always to think of the other person as more important than I. Remember that these verses were addressed historically to fellow believers. Certainly some of the Christians in the church of Philippi were more gifted than others, and some were carrying more of the work load than others, and some were more spiritual-acting than others. And yet God's directive in that situation was for everyone to regard every other fellow believer as the more important person. You can be sure that if we were to follow this line of thinking, the problem of pride would be checked and we would have minds more in control. A proud Christian may look like he has it all together, but unchecked pride always ripples out to other people in hurt waves and is a sure sign of a mind out of control before God.

We must also *conquer prejudice* toward others in our program of mind control. This responsibility emerges from Philippians 4:8 when this verse is seen against the background of the entire letter to the Philippians. One of the reasons why the apostle Paul wrote this letter was that a rift was beginning to take place in the Philippian fellowship. The cause is unknown, but it was not a major doctrinal problem. Apparently it was a minor matter on which the church could not agree. In any case, it seems that the friction was causing personal rivalries and bad feelings among the Philippian believers. Two zealous women named Euodia and Syntyche were particularly involved (verses 2-3). Paul knew very well that molehills can become mountains and therefore throughout the Epistle he urged the Philippians to show unselfish love to one another. (Look, for example, at the context of the well-known Christological passage in Philippians 2:1-11).

In Philippians 4 the exhortation toward unity continues. The Philippian Christians were to work at forbearance (self-restraint when provoked) with all the members of the fellowship (verse 5). They were not to become tense about present circumstances, even when things in the fellowship were not going their way (verse 6). Peace of mind and heart through prayer, not manipulative persuasion of others, was the way (verses 6-7). And now in verse 8, a final suggestion is given to the Philippians to help them along the road to greater unity. They should think positively about one another—and so should we. Let us not fix our thoughts on the faults of fellow believers but on their good points. Let us focus on whatever is noble and honorable about the brother who rubs us the wrong way; there must be something true and right about him. Let us think about whatever is pure and lovable in the sister who talked behind our back; she must have some admirable quality. If there is even the faintest glimmer of excellence or even the smallest item worthy of praise, then let our minds dwell on these things. Every believer has weaknesses as well as strengths—even you! But if we make a definite effort to think about the strengths of the person and not focus on the negatives, we will find that we are able to conquer our prejudices about our fellow believers. Try drawing up a list of positives for every person that is bothering you right now and see how this results in greater control of your thoughts about other people. This type of mind control brings not only peace to your fellowship but the presence of God to your soul (verse 7), because to conquer prejudice is to please the God of peace (verse 9).

A further principle of mind control, seen in 1 Peter 1:13, is to *cultivate priorities*. To gird up the mind for action means to be disciplined in thinking. This expression comes from Bible days, when the people gathered up or girded up their long garments for un-impeded activity. Too many side interests can impede and interfere with our thinking priorities as growing Christians. In view of our great salvation (verses 3-12), we should therefore discipline our minds to set our priorities accordingly. How much time do we waste thinking about things that are not going to matter one hundred years from now—or even one year from now? Why not control our minds to think more about eternal realities as this verse commands us? The point here is not that we are never to think about styles or stocks or superbowls or other temporal things, but rather that we need to cultivate the habit of thinking more about what really matters. Maybe we should start by cultivating the priority of spending some time alone with the Lord every day, reading His Word and speaking to Him in prayer. A regular quiet time with God is not the easiest habit to maintain, but such disci-plined control of our minds is of primary importance because it leads to practicing all the other principles of mind control. Remember: your mind matters. Keep it in control!

39

Disappointments and Appointments

Genesis 50:20   As for you, you meant evil
against me, but God meant it for good in
order to bring about this present result, to
preserve many people alive.
*Read the whole account of the life of Joseph
in Genesis 37-50.*

"Our disappointments are God's appointments" is one of those well-known Christian clichés.
Unfortunately we sometimes become desensitized to
the truth of much quoted sayings because of their fa-
miliarity. The above statement is not only true but very
important, and we need to constantly remind ourselves
that God really is in control of our disappointments.
Maybe you had a disappointing year—a boring job or
a broken love relationship. Perhaps you are disappointed right now—a frustrating teacher or a two-
faced "friend." Remember that God is sovereign and
knows all about your situation. He has actually ap-

pointed you to all these disappointments for any of several good reasons.

The story of Joseph is a classic example of how God used disappointments in a young believer's life to accomplish His own good purposes. Genesis 50:20 gives us the conclusion of the story in Joseph's own words. Joseph recognized that the disappointments which he had experienced (even evil at the hands of his own family) were miraculously woven together by God to preserve many lives from starvation in the ancient world. What super faith Joseph exhibited when he stated: "God meant it for good." Can we say the same? Is our faith strong enough to recognize that God not only permits disappointments to come our way but also appoints them? (See Romans 8:28-29 in this connection.)

The first big disappointment in Joseph's life came when he was seventeen years old. We read about this in Genesis 37. Joseph's brothers sold him as a slave to some bedouin traders who were on their way to Egypt. A number of things led up to this disappointment in Joseph's life, possibly including his own failings. We read that Jacob, Joseph's father, had played favorites with his sons. He gave Joseph a beautiful and expensive robe (verses 3-4). Jacob should have known that this display of favoritism might cause friction in the family. Parents run the same risk today when they play favorites with their children. We also learn that Joseph apparently assumed a superior attitude toward his brothers which further aroused their hatred and jealousy. Not only did teenager Joseph keep tabs on his older brothers (verse 2) but he seems to have lost no time in relating his dreams to them, dreams in which he was the "hero" (verses 5-11). Now it is true that God was behind these dreams and they all would eventually come true. However, at this point maybe Joseph should have kept these dreams to himself. But let's not belittle Joseph without recognizing that we are guilty of similar failings. How often we assume a superior attitude and look down on people whom we think have less intelligence, less charisma, less money, less natural talent, or even less spiritual gift. How illogical and wrong! Everything we have has been given to us. "What do you have that you did not receive?" (1 Corinthians 4:7).

The most amazing and wonderful lesson for us in this part of the Joseph narrative is that God takes not only our disappointments but even our failings and works them into His overall good purposes for us and others. Of course this does not excuse us for our faults or make God guilty of evil in any way, but it does indicate that our sovereign God can overrule in the area of our mistakes. We can be sure that in the resulting pattern of events, God will work things together so that we are disciplined and taught and led to maturity in the very areas where we failed. Joseph must have thought more than once about his attitude toward his brothers as he lay in that empty cistern (Genesis 37:24) awaiting the unknown. Being sold as a slave to a camel caravan was not exactly an ego trip for Joseph! The Lord would yet teach Joseph how to properly use his God-given abilities in the area of dreams (see Genesis 40 and 41).

Another important lesson for us from the life of Joseph concerns faithfulness. Joseph had his rough edges, but throughout the disappointments in his life we never once read of Joseph falling from faith or speaking out against God. Our reaction in similar circumstances would probably be, "Why me, God? How could You allow my own family to treat me like this?" Joseph's faithfulness through disappointments puts many of us to shame.

The next big disappointment in Joseph's life came when he was in Egypt. In Genesis 39 we learn that Joseph was falsely accused and thrown into prison. What led up to this disappointment? Joseph had become the slave of an Egyptian official named Potiphar. He had served well and had been elevated to the position of head servant. Scripture (Genesis 39:1-5) leaves no doubt that God was sovereignly working behind the scenes. Things seemed to be going reasonably well, but then came a critical test in the life of Joseph.

Joseph was a good-looking and well-built man (verse 6) and Potiphar's wife tried to seduce him. What a temptation for Joseph—away from home and the restraining eye of his family; in pagan Egypt where "everyone does it"; bursting with all the sexual energy of a healthy young man; seemingly forsaken by God and in desperate need of some companionship. Why not? Who would know? But (verse 8) Joseph refused and remained faithful to the Lord. He recognized that this act would be sin against his master Potiphar and his wife—and against God (verse 9). The fact that Joseph had unfairly been made a slave did not make it any less sin. And the possibility that Potiphar's wife might have been lonely and needing love did not make it any less sin either. Situation ethics do not apply! If the Bible espoused situation ethics this would be the ideal place for God to teach it—but He doesn't!

The test of Joseph's faith was not a onetime temptation. It came day after day (verse 10). Would we have remained faithful? Perhaps some of us would even have jumped to the false conclusion that such a prolonged "open door" was actually God's way of meeting our needs in a difficult situation. No! God never leads us or meets our needs in ways that are contrary to His Word.

Before leaving Joseph's test of faith let us look at two other lessons. First, notice that the test revolved around Joseph's own God-given good looks. Potiphar's wife just would not have been interested in a fat, ugly Joseph! How often the tests of our faith center around the good things God has given us, even the wonderful spiritual gifts that God graciously gives. Notice, too, the method of victory over this type of temptation: actually running away physically. Joseph didn't stand around to see how long he could resist the propositions of a beautiful woman. He got away from the situation as quickly as possible. This is the scriptural method of victory over the "lusts of the flesh." Don't hang around such tempting situations to show your faith, but rather get away (immediately!) from these situations to prove your faith.

As a result of his faithfulness, Joseph was falsely accused and convicted of being a rapist. How could God allow such a horrible disappointment? Remember that God allowed the horrible butchery of the cross in order to save us from our sins. We can be sure that if our God allows a deep disappointment to come into our lives, He has appointed us to this disappointment for some good reason. We may not understand the "why" until eternity. This takes a measure of faith beyond the ordinary, but God provides the means to cope in such cases. (See 2 Corinthians 12:7-10.)

Joseph's vindication fianlly came, but not before another major disappointment. While in jail, Joseph came in contact with two officials of Pharaoh, the king of all Egypt (Genesis 40). Note again how the sovereignty of God was at work in bringing them to the "same place where Joseph was imprisoned" (verse 3). The two officials had dreams which Joseph correctly interpreted. Joseph asked Pharaoh's cupbearer to remember him when the cupbearer was released from prison and restored to office. Naturally the official forgot all about Joseph when he went back to the court of Pharaoh. Did anyone ever take advantage of your generosity and then ignore you as if you didn't exist anymore? We can imagine the disappointment for Joseph. Expectations were dashed. Why not give up? Surely God must have forgotten about him wasting prime years in that miserable Egyptian prison—if there even was a God! At least two years went by with no change. Have you even been in that miserable, disappointing rut? From our perspective there seems to be no action, only wasted time. From God's perspective it may be an appointment in which to learn patience and humility and other reasons too.

In Genesis 41 we have the story of Joseph's exaltation. The cupbearer was finally forced to remember Joseph when God gave Pharaoh a couple of dreams. Joseph was released from prison and brought before the king of Egypt to interpret his dreams. But Joseph's first words before Pharaoh were about God. The Scripture leaves no doubt that Joseph had remained faithful to God throughout his entire incarceration and fully intended to remain faithful before this pagan ruler. Would we be as faithful, or would we decide somewhere along the line to change allegiance? God honored Joseph for his faithfulness. He was elevated to second in command over all Egypt. Such a position for a Hebrew young man required all the experience of Egyptian life and government that Joseph had learned during those years of disappointment. God knew what He was doing all along. He still does! Our disappointments are God's appointments!

40

Why Me, Lord?

Job 7:19-20, NIV   Will You never look away
from me, or let me alone even for an instant?
If I have sinned, what have I done to You, O
watcher of men? Why have You made me Your
target? Have I become a burden to You?

"Why me, Lord?" Have you ever asked God
that question? Let's admit it, we've all probably voiced
that question at one time or another (or at least
thought it) especially during times of extreme pressure
or pain. More than three thousand years ago there was
a man named Job who, when he was experiencing
great suffering, asked God that question. And God answered him. God's answer to Job is recorded in the
Old Testament book of Job, which was written for our
benefit (Romans 15:4). Let's look at the ancient story
of Job and carefully examine God's answer to see how
it applies to our "Why me?" questions today.

"Why me, Lord?" is really part of a much larger
question that is wrestled with in the book of Job. How

can a good God of love and mercy, who is also all-knowing and all-powerful, allow suffering, especially the suffering of innocent and righteous people? Is this characteristic of a just and fair God? A defense of God's goodness and omnipotence in light of such apparent inconsistencies is known as a theodicy. The book of Job serves as a theodicy, a vindication of God in spite of the sufferings of poor, innocent Job.

The particular aspect of suffering that is dealt with in this book is the purpose of suffering in the life of the believer. The complete answer covering every detail of the complex problem of suffering is not the intention of this book of Scripture. In Job we see that God allows suffering in order to accomplish His good purposes in our lives. Here again, the book of Job is not an exhaustive treatment of the many ways in which God uses suffering for our good. However, three sure answers to the question "Why me, Lord?" clearly emerge from a brief study of the book of Job.

The first and most obvious reason for Job's suffering was for God to *diagnose Job's faith*. The Bible teaches that God tests the faith of believers to prove its genuine quality. 1 Peter 1:7 states that a proven faith is worth far more than gold and results in praise, glory, and honor to God. God's testing of our faith is similar to a father proving his young son's character by purposely putting him into situations around the home where he is forced to bear some burdens—not just play all the time. How pleased and honored the father is to see his son respond correctly even in difficult circumstances. In the first two chapters of Job we see God permitting circumstances which severely tested Job's faith. At the beginning of chapter 1 Job was a man of great wealth and influence and a man of outstanding faith. God's diagnosis of Job and his faith at this point is given in Job 1:1: blameless and upright, fearing God and turning away from evil. Could God make this statement about our faith and character?

As we follow the story of Job we see two giant waves of adversity sweep unexpectedly over the patriarch and leave him struggling to believe. In the first wave Job lost all his children and all his possessions. Think of the magnitude of such a loss! It makes many of our "why me?" outbursts seem completely out of place. In spite of such a tragic loss, Job recognized the truth that everything we have in this life comes from the gracious hand of God. Job worshiped the Lord, saying, "The Lord gave and the Lord has taken away; may the name of the Lord be praised" (Job 1:20-21). The diagnosis of Job's faith after this first wave of affliction is given in verse 22. "In all this, Job did not sin by charging God with wrongdoing."

The second wave of suffering came even closer to home. Job's own body was afflicted. He was covered with painful boils (Job 2:7). His skin was crusty and oozed serum that attracted worms (Job 7:5). There was no relief from the fever and intense pain that he was experiencing (Job 2:13; 30:17,30). What kind of faith in God would we exhibit under these horrible conditions? Job's response could only come from a deeply rooted faith in God. "Shall we accept good from God, and not trouble?" Again God's diagnosis of Job's tested faith is given in Job 2:10. "In all this, Job did not sin in what he said."

God had more in mind than just a diagnosis of Job's faith when He allowed His servant to suffer. He also wanted to *develop Job's faith*. Yes, even the faith of patient Job needed some maturing. While Job did not renounce God throughout his ordeal, he did raise the question of "Why me, Lord?" (See Job 7:19-20). In fact, from chapters 3–31 we see that Job's constant response to the counsel of his three friends was essentially, "Why me?" Job could not understand why God was letting all this happen to him. Did God really know what He was doing? Eliphaz, Bildad, and Zophar thought they knew. Their logic was simple. "All suffering is the result of sin. Job is suffering; therefore Job has sinned." But Job staunchly maintained his innocence. On this point Job was right and his counselors were wrong. That's why they, and not Job, had to bring sacrifices in the end (Job 42:7-9). But Job was wrong for questioning God's ways and having a "why me" attitude. This is the area where Job's faith needed to be developed–and ours does too!

In chapters 32–37, Elihu, a fourth counselor, came closer to the truth than Job's first three counselors. Elihu told Job that he was being disciplined by God and that Job should submit to God instead of questioning Him. It appears that God used Elihu to pave the way for His own answer to Job. It is noteworthy that Elihu did not have to bring sacrifices in the end and also that Job was silent and listening through all of Elihu's speeches.

Finally, the Lord spoke directly to Job. God's answer took the wind right out of Job's sails! By a series of questions the Lord gave Job a small glimpse of His infinite knowledge and power. Who was Job—a mere fledgling, a finite creature—to question the ways of the almighty and sovereign Creator? Job was reduced to the level of a kindergarten child. It was like a proud and loud-mouthed high school algebra student, who thinks he has the last word in math, suddenly being confronted by Einstein. However, Job's response was beautiful, and it was evidence of a great step in the development of his faith. (See Job 40:3-5; 42:1-6.) Job recognized his insignificance and ignorance. He retracted his former "why me?" statements and repented of his wrong attitude. He realized that the Lord could see the big picture and was in control of everything, including his suffering. He humbly submitted to the hand of God and awaited further instruction. Job had taken a giant leap forward in his faith.

God wants to develop our faith also. "Why me, Lord?" is not blasphemy, but it is a sign of immaturity and actually is a sign of our subconscious pride in our own self-righteousness! To question the ways of God in our lives with an unsubmissive attitude or the idea that God is unfair and doesn't quite know what He's doing is really the basic sin of pride. It is evidence of a faith that needs to grow and develop and come to a proper understanding of who God is. During times of smooth sailing we often feel self-satisfied and even judge others. Paradoxically, it is through the "why me?" situations that our wrong attitudes begin to change. A growing Christian learns to humbly submit to the hand of God and to trust His inscrutable ways. Is your faith being developed?

God's response in Job's suffering was also to *display Job's faith.* Job was God's "Exhibit A"—not only to earthly people but to heavenly beings as well. In Job 1:6-8 and 2:1-3 it is quite obvious from the Lord's questions to Satan that Job's faith was on display before the unseen world. Although Job's faith was not perfect and was in the process of being developed, God still took delight in pointing out the faith of His servant. Can God take delight in the display of our faith?

The fact that the angelic hosts (both good and bad) are observing the evidence of our faith should motivate us to a more consistent Christian walk. Remember that Satan is called "the accuser" of believers. (See Zechariah 3:1 and Revelation 12:10.) Unfortunately, the enemy of our souls usually has lots of evidence from our lives that he can use for accusation.

In connection with the display of our faith it is comforting to know that God will never permit a situation in which our suffering is so great that our faith has to fail. Notice that God set limits on how much heat Satan was allowed to bring to Job's crucible of life (Job 1:12; 2:6). 1 Corinthians 10:13 assures us that God still sets the limits as to how much heat can be applied to our lives. The protective hedge that was around Job (Job 1:10) is around us as well. It is lowered only when the Lord knows we're strong enough to handle the situation.

The last chapter of Job shows the happy scene of Job's restoration. God's purposes through suffering were effected in Job and he was blessed. We too will know the blessing of God in our lives forever, as we come to understand now God's answer to, "Why me, Lord?"

Acknowledgments

First of all, my thanks must go to my forbearing wife, Margie, for her many helpful suggestions and her many hours of manuscript typing. Each mini-study was typed at least twice in the editing process.

Thanks are also extended to my mother-in-law, Mrs. John Smart, for reading every devotional and making helpful editing suggestions.

I am grateful to my children, Cathie, David, and Ron, who have patiently endured the monthly inundation of our home with five thousand copies of our monthly newsletter, which is the origin of this collection of devotional studies. They, along with many of our "arm-twisted" friends, have often helped with collating and stuffing envelopes.

Finally, I am indebted to Mr. William MacDonald for his gracious words in the foreword of this book.

David R. Reid

ABOUT THE AUTHOR ...

David R. Reid (B.S., Ph.D., Rutgers University:
M.T.S., Gordon-Conwell Theological Seminary)
is currently a member of the faculty at Emmaus
Bible College, Dubuque, Iowa. In addition to
his teaching and preaching responsibilities,
Dr. Reid also writes a monthly newsletter which
is mailed to Christians worldwide.